Herd & Mackenzie

The Story of a Shipyard

HIE Moray

Our thanks for the financial support received for the production of this book from HIE Moray

Herd & Mackenzie

The Story of a Shipyard

By

John Addison - John Crawford
Jim Farquhar - Ron Stewart

Published by
Buckie & District Fishing Heritage Centre Ltd.

ISBN 978-0-9556241-0-0

Buckie & District Fishing Heritage Centre Ltd

The Buckie & District Fishing Heritage Centre Ltd is a registered charity committed to preserving the history of the local area.

There are no paid staff whatsoever, every person involved in the running of the Centre are volunteers, many in their late years of life. Their knowledge of the local area is second to none; their knowledge of the sea is second to none. They are experienced men and women who continue to play their part in the fabric of the local society.

The Centre has a vast collection of photographs and artefacts, locally published booklets on all aspects of the Fishing Heritage of the area. They run educational visits for local schoolchildren and in the recently extended and refurbished 'Cottage 'it is hoped to extend this aspect of Heritage.

The aim is to continue to provide an educational and historical resource for all those interested in the rich history of the fishing that built the local communities along the Moray Coast.

The Buckie & District Fishing Heritage Centre is adjacent to the Library in Cluny Place, Buckie, car parking is available.

Acknowledgements

Many of the photographs in this book have been taken from the extensive collection of over 7,000 photographs held by the Buckie & District Fishing Heritage Society Ltd. The remainder come from the private collection of John Addison. Larger copies of photographs featured in the book that belong to the Society can be purchased from the Cottage or by writing to the secretary at the Cottage. The photographs of BCK 142 Celerity on page 106 and of MFV 1043 (Kathleen Pirie) on page 109 were kindly loaned by the Malcolm White Collection.

Other information on launchings & boat histories have been gleaned from back copies of the Banffshire Advertiser, Olson's Almanacs and Files within The Heritage Centre which unfortunately do not stipulate the previous author's names and therefore we offer our apologies for the lack of acknowledgements.

We are indebted to John H Mackenzie who worked extremely hard and with great enthusiasm on the project before he passed away. Thanks also to his family for their continued support in the project by providing material and photographs.

Any mistakes or further omissions are the sole responsibility of the authors.

Introduction

By

Jim Farquhar

This was to be the "Boss's" pages; his words would introduce this project which had filled him with pride. It was to give him the opportunity to praise the men and women who had worked in the yard over the years.

Sadly, it was not to be as he passed away before he could write his introduction. It has fallen to me to carry out the task that I know he would have taken great pleasure in completing.

The pride that the Boss had for the Yard went far beyond the perimeter boundary as he told us when we were obtaining information from him for this book, Herd and Mackenzie had a workforce capable of building any type of vessel, as he told all who came to his office looking to build. The amount of men and apprentices that went through the yard and went on to further their knowledge gave him great satisfaction and pride. He was always keen to hear from them in future years How 'His Loons' had progressed, after leaving the Yard.

He was proud of his forebears who started the yard from nothing and built it up to a thriving business through the First World War, the depression and the Second World War.

After the war the Boss went looking for work to Whitehall, as the fishing industry had not fully recovered after the war, and came back with Admiralty work which allowed him to build up the workforce to around 250 employees.

The name of Herd & Mackenzie became known throughout the world as a builder of fine vessels. The Boss always said each vessel he built had always to be the strongest, safest and finest to meet the needs of those who went to face the elements of the waters around our coastline.

His pride in the Yard and its workforce throughout the years earned him the respect and admiration of all the people with whom he came in contact.

John Herd Mackenzie was great boat builder with foresight, an astute businessman, a respected employer, and a tireless worker in the Boatbuilding Industry and most of all a great man.

The people of the area and all over will always remember the name of HERD & MACKENZIE, Shipbuilders & Engineers, Buckie, Scotland.

A dream is born...

On 3rd October 1873 in Ludgate Place, Alloa, Clackmannan, Thomas Mackenzie came into the world at 11 a.m. His father Thomas Mackenzie and mother Elizabeth Graham had married some two years earlier at Blair Cottage, Oakley, in the parish of Carnock in Fife on 8th December 1871. His mother, Elizabeth was the daughter of John Graham and Elizabeth Thomson. The grandfather of young Thomas was Peter Mackenzie a joiner, his grandmother was Jane Wright.

On 31st October 1877 at 0130 hours James Herd was born at 9 Leven Street, Dumbarton, the son of John Herd and Margaret Stronach who had married at 10 Leven Street, Dumbarton on 31st December 1874. Margaret Stronach hailed from Lossiemouth and was the daughter of George Stronach a Master seaman and Ann Young. The young infant's father, John Herd, was the son of James Herd and Margaret Sutherland.

James Herd and Margaret Sutherland had a number of children all born in the parish of Rathven, Banff.

1. William Herd   born 8th February 1832
2. James Herd   born 25th February 1834
3. Robert Herd   born 20th July 1837
4. Ann Herd   born 1st July 1839
5. Adam Herd   born 15th August 1841
6. John Herd   born 5th June 1847. Married to Margaret Stronach
7. George Herd   born 15th July 1849.

On 27th October 1899 Thomas Mackenzie was married, he was a 26 years old Shipwright and lived at 100 Glasgow Road, Dumbarton, his wife was Margaret Ann Herd a 23 years old daughter of John Herd and Margaret Stronach, her father was a Shipwright who lived at Boundary Street, Dumbarton.

Thomas Mackenzie worked at Denny's shipyard alongside his wife's father and her brother James and his wife's uncle Adam Herd's son, William Herd. All were shipwrights in Denny's.

Denny's Shipyard was perhaps the most famous of the yards on the River Clyde. Denny's is still a going concern and occupies a prime spot in the centre of the town of Dumbarton. Easily the most famous ship built there was the *Cutty Sark*, which was finished in 1869 at a cost of £16.150. She became very well known worldwide and is still an extremely popular visitor attraction with more than 15 million visitors boarding the ship at Greenwich.

On 25th December 1901 William Herd was a 26 years old Shipwright and lived at Edindoune Cottage, Dumbarton, he was employed at Denny's shipyard and was the son of Adam Herd (a Shipwright) and Elizabeth Hendry. He married Catherine Colquhoun McLaren who lived at 1 Castlegreen Street, Dumbarton and was the daughter of John McLaren and Helen Renwick.

Two days later on 27th December 1901 James Herd a 24 years old Shipwright of Cairndhu Cottage, Boundary Street, Dumbarton and the son of John Herd (shipwright) and Margaret Stronach (who was deceased by the time of her son's wedding) married Martha Rodger of 89 Glasgow Road, Dumbarton the daughter of William Rodger (Shipwright) and Martha McFadyen.

With such a proliferation of shipwrights in the family, it was almost a certainty that the three young men who formed the first company of W & J Herd and Mackenzie would have the skills in their hands and in their blood to be able to build bonny boats and to pass their skills to others for the future.

The Cutty Sark that Denny's built with such pride was held in high esteem as the crowning glory of the skills garnered at Denny's. Perhaps this ship crafted by such skilled shipwrights was also a factor in the ability of the Herd & Mackenzie yard many decades later to strive to have the skills on their work force to build the Captain Scott – an equally fine sailing ship of the modern era.

On the 21st March 1911, John Herd Mackenzie was born in Findochty and it was he who was destined to carry on with the traditions built by his father and his kin.

As a young man, he was unfortunate to be involved in a motor cycle accident, which left him with one leg shorter than the other by a couple of inches. This did not hold him up for one minute as he ploughed through life like one of the fishing boats he launched ploughed through the waves for year after year.

John H Mackenzie and Mary Bunyan on their wedding day.

On 31st October 1946, Margaret Ann Herd the wife of Thomas Mackenzie died at Allandale Enzie. She was 70 years of age.

James Herd was the first of the two original partners to die. He died aged 73 at Cairndhu, Findochty on 13th February 1951.

Some months later, Thomas Mackenzie died on 24th October 1951 at Garmoyle in Findochty he was 78 years of age. His son John registered his death.

Not without some trepidation, John Herd Mackenzie stepped into the shoes of the men who had built the company to a high standard. He carried on the traditions started by his father and uncles all those years before. It was under his stewardship that the company built the Captain Scott, a sailing ship in the best traditions of the Cutty Sark.

The yard went from strength to strength under 'Johnny 'as he was universally known. He searched far and wide into ever increasing stormy waters to get work for his men and his yard in Buckie.

John Herd Mackenzie

The onset of time finally forced John Mackenzie to retire and let younger men take over the responsibilities for the yard. The yard was sold and he retired.

Even though he had stepped back from the yard, he was still very interested in what they were building at the yard and what all the craftsmen he knew so well were doing with themselves.

John's dear wife Mary died on 16th April 1989 and was a sad loss to bear for John and family.

He finally moved to a house in Banchory, he was not getting any younger and eventually he was confined to a wheelchair that proved to be a nuisance to him, his brain was as keen and as sharp as it ever was. His family visited often and he was in touch with various people from the Buckie area. He devoured any information he could find of his old yard and news of 'his' men of whom he had thought the world.

In the late autumn of 2006, the Buckie & District Fishing Heritage thought it would be a good idea to write a story about the yard from its start to its ultimate end and featuring all the boats built there during the time it was Herd & Mackenzie yard. All the villages in the area had at least one boat built for one of its fishermen.

Needless to say Johnny was very excited when he found out about the proposed project and threw open his doors and his historical artefacts to the small group working on the story. He looked forward to the visits as he was grilled mercilessly for his memories. He was a willing horse and wrote constantly in his own inimitable fashion, tiny precise writing that was difficult to read because of its tiny letters but legible nevertheless.

Sadly Johnny Mackenzie died on 13th January 2007 before the story could be published.

His memories will be stamped throughout the story and his notes have been drawn on heavily to try and put over the human face behind the yard.

He called his inquisitors the 'Three Wise Men', another pointer if any were needed, to the type of person he was and his sense of humour.

He loved the banter as questions were fired at him from all three for hours on end, he would pick on a subject and off he would go, only to be pulled back in order to get these memories down on paper.

During the visits his daughter, Grace, was on hand to referee the contests and to fuss around us making sure we had what we needed and to take charge of things when we went for lunch to the local golf club. John knew all of the staff there and always had a word for each of them as they came to greet him on his arrival with his guests.

There is little doubt that the man himself will be remembered with great fondness in the town of Findochty, where he had been a one time provost and of course in Buckie where through his efforts many men were provided with work over a long period of time. He will be sadly missed for his enthusiasm shown to the project and his seemingly boundless energy in the long sessions he hosted just before his death.

Herd & Mackenzie

A Brief History

It was the turn of the last century, 1900, when the idea of a shipbuilding yard at Buckie came about.   Thomas Mackenzie, a ships carpenter, and his wife were on holiday at Findochty.   They had recently been married; Tom was a shipwright at Denny Shipbuilding Yard in Dumbarton.   As they looked down at the Moray Firth from the Kirk Brae, Tom turned to his wife and said, "I'm coming back here to build ships'.   He was referring to an inlet of the sea known locally as Crooked Hythe.

On his return to Dumbarton, he approached William Herd, his wife's cousin and James Herd who was his wife's brother and told them what he had in mind.   Both William and James were shipwrights and they readily agreed to join him.

> *Fifty three years ago two enterprising young men with an unshakeable faith in the future of building fishing boats for the district and a grim determination to make good, carved a slipway out of the rocky coast at Crooked Hythe Findochty.*
>
> *Sceptics wrote off their ideas as fanciful, attributing them to youthful exuberance which would soon be curbed by the bitter school of experience. Their proposals to slip and refit fishing boats on such a humble and almost primitive slipway would never work, said the critics.*
>
> *Undeterred, the two young men worked away quietly, never wavering from their purpose and from that tiny, crudely-fashioned slipway to which they gave birth has grown in little over half a century to the vast sprawling mass of buildings, workshops and slipways that is today the headquarters at Buckie of the ship building firm of Messrs Herd and Mackenzie.*
>
> *For the two men, relatives by marriage were James Herd and Thomas Mackenzie, founders of a firm which has a proud reputation and record of achievement in the country's ship-building circles.[1]*

They applied for and were granted a lease of the ground at Crooked Hythe from the Dowager Countess of Seafield and arranged to move north.   The three men were in their twenties and all had just married and had started families.

---

[1] Banffshire Advertiser 29th March 1956

Crooked Hythe was eminently suitable for the slipway. It was a natural harbour, sheltered from all winds, and was the only suitable harbour for ships and boats trading with Findochty prior to 1884. The nearest slip was at Banff, and this was altogether inadequate for the increasing demand for slipways in the area.

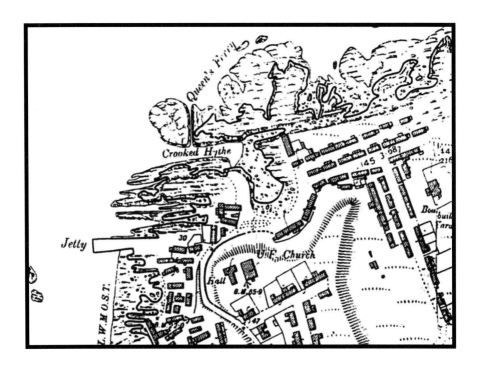

The above map shows the location of the Crooked Hythe at Findochty, a natural choice for a slipway that is sheltered and has ready access to the sea.

The early years of the 20th Century was a time when the steam drifter began to replace the old "Zulu" and "Fifie" sail-boats in the Moray Firth fishing ports.

As the new type of craft found favour among the fishermen, it became apparent that the change-over would be rapid. The young brothers in law, carpenters with Dennys of Dumbarton, one of the most famous shipyards in the country, accurately assessed the possibilities and the probable demand for a locally-built vessel and slipping facilities. From an early age the building of ships has fascinated them and here was the great chance to realise their ambition to branch out on their own.[2]

---

[2] Taken from Banffshire Advertiser article 29th March 1956

They arrived at Findochty on 23rd April 1903. The first job was to form a slipway capable of taking vessels up to 90 feet in length. They worked all daylight hours available at the backbreaking work and completed the slipway in December 1903.

During the first year operations were confined to the construction of the slipway and carriage and the installation of the winch gear. Success rewarded the care and diligence put into the preparatory work for, in spite of local disbelief, a fishing boat was duly slipped, refitted, painted and successfully re-launched.[3]

The passage through the rocks to the slipway had an awkward bend hence the name Crooked Hythe, it made for skilled manoeuvrability by the skippers of the large Zulu boats which would need to pick their way to the slipway.

Many skippers were reluctant to attempt it until one, James Mair, a local skipper from Portknockie just along the coast, brought his Zulu Valkyrie (BF1947) through the channel without mishap on 4th December 1903. The Zulu was a sailing boat the design of which was greatly admired as they were good sea boats and sailed well.

When the *Valkyrie* overhaul was successfully finished, the slipway was suddenly in demand for the repair and repainting of the Zulu boats and the Steam Drifters. It would be a matter of pride among the fiercely competitive fishing boat skippers that no skipper wanted to be seen as not being skilful enough to navigate to the slipway.

---

[3] Ibid

Zulu boat Valkyrie BF 1947 on slipway. Could the men on the ground be the original
Messrs Herd & Mackenzie?

The notice board reads as follows:-

Herd &
Mackenzie
Slipway
Findochty
04. 12. 03

The first advertisement was in the Banffshire Advertiser of 7th January 1904 stating that W & J Herd & Mackenzie (Mackenzie was spelt wrongly) had completed a slipway and was now open to take all kinds of new building and repair work.

IMPORTANT NOTICE TO FISHERMEN.

Messrs W. & J. Herd & M'Kenzie,

BOATBUILDERS, FINDOCHTY,

BEG to announce to Fishermen and others that they have completed the ERECTION OF A SLIP-WAY in connection with Building Yard, and every facility is now provided for the prompt REPAIR and Cleaning of all CLASSES of Fishing Vessels.

WOODEN STEAM DRIFTERS BUILT ON REASONABLE TERMS.

Advertisement on front page of Banffshire Advertiser
Dated Thursday January 7th 1904

The fishermen in the Buckie area were the pioneers of steam drifters on the Moray Firth and in 1903 they had about 25 drifters most of which had been built in England

Buckie was an important herring port and in 1903 had landed 2815 tons of herring. It had to increase its efficiency as a herring port and that meant building more steam drifters. W & J Herd and Mackenzie were at the forefront of that drive to build wooden steam drifters locally and provide facilities for their overhaul when required.

William Herd then decided to return to the Clyde. The firms name changed to reflect this change and thereafter was Herd & Mackenzie.

The workforce at Findochty

The first order for a new build was received in November 1905, the original order book entry shows the following;-

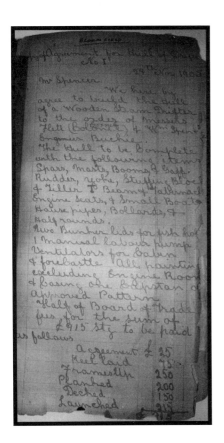

Original entry in order book

Transliteration of the column opposite

Bloomfield

Copy of Agreement for Hull of Ship No 1

29th Nov 1905

Mr Spencer,

 We hereby agree to build the Hull of a Wooden Steam Drifter to the order of Messrs Flett 'Cornel' & Wm. Spencer, Engineer, Buckie.

The Hull to be Complete with the following items;-
Spars, masts, boom and gaff, rudder, yoke, staffing block and tiller.   Beam and tabernacle, engine seats and small boat, hawse pipes, bollards and half rounds.
Two bunker lids for fish hold.   1 manual labour pump.   Ventilators for cabin & forecastle.   All painting excluding engine room and casing.   One capstan of approved pattern.   Half of Board of Trade fees for the sum of £915 stg. to be paid as follows

Agreement	£25
Keel laid	£75
Frames up	£250
Planked	£200
Decked	£150
Launched	£215
	£915.

Towards the end of 1905, the firm received their first order for a steam drifter and early in 1906, the Steam Drifter *Bloomfield* was launched no doubt with great pride and not a little relief by the two partners and their workforce. They were probably one of the main boat builders in the area and with their ready access to the sea were in a good position to build on their reputation very quickly. The boat builders worked out in the open air and had no shelter from the elements, they could perhaps show some empathy for the fishermen for whom they build the boats.

> *That vessel cost only £915 to build excluding engine and boilers with the weekly wage bill at the yard averaging £15 - a startling contrast to the present cost of around £12000 for the modern, much smaller, motor fishing boat and weekly wage bills running into many hundreds of pounds.*

> *The success with the Bloomfield had obviously been carefully noted; orders began to trickle in and two more vessels were launched during that year. The trickle became a flow and in 1907 four were sent into the water at the Crooked Hythe while in the years up to the outbreak of the First World War in 1914, launchings averaged three a year.[4]*

2 boats building at Crooked Hythe Findochty in the early days

---

[4] Taken from Banffshire Advertiser article 29th March 1956

Vallar Crown BF 249 under tow from SD Rose after Launching 1906

Between 1905 and 1915, 32 Steam Drifters, mostly 90ft long, were built at Findochty; the majority were fitted with triple expansion engines made by John Lewis of Aberdeen and boilers made by Dalgleish of Glasgow.

James Herd
Born 31st October 1877 - Died 13th February 1951

Thomas Mackenzie
Born 3rd October 1873 – Died 24th October 1951

The First World War brought a new challenge to the fishermen of Great Britain; they were drafted in to assist the Royal Navy, their boats were converted from

fishing to fighting. Their main task was to act as anti-submarine vessels. Herd &
Mackenzie was working flat out doing conversions and building steam drifters to
the specifications of the Admiralty.

Many men from the area volunteered themselves to serve in the Navy, they were
highly skilled seamen and they were more than welcome. Their boats were
commandeered to join in the fight against the might of the German Navy and its
allies.

Casualties among the fishermen who went to war were heavy; they lost their
lives and their boats during the war. Drifters built by Herd & Mackenzie during
this period for the Admiralty were the *Silt*, the *Solstice* and the *Sunspot*. Of
particular interest to Herd & Mackenzie was the reported death in March 1918 of
Private John Gauld M.M. of the 6th Gordon Highlanders who was killed in action in
France. He was aged 22 years and before the war was a clerk with Herd &
Mackenzie.

At the end of the war the yard was even busier, many boats were brought in for
repair after their war duties, many had to be stripped of their wartime gear and
returned to normal fishing vessels. This meant that there was little space
available for work that had to be undertaken.

The 'new' Buckie Harbour was completed and the Council invited tenders for the
slipway sites in the East Basin. After protracted discussions it was finally agreed
that Site Number 1 next to the North Pier would go to Jones; Herd and Mackenzie
would go to Site number 2 and George Smith would go to Site Number 3 next to
Commercial Road.

Herd & Mackenzie wasted no time in accepting the site offer and immediately
started constructing a slipway. Eventually both Jones and George Smith gave up
their sites. Herd & Mackenzie stepped in, took over both, and eventually had all
the ground from the north pier to the roadway and the ground at the south side

of the railway embankment. The slipway was built to take vessels of 150 feet long and with a displacement of 400 tons.

Just after the new yard at Buckie opened for business, the owners decided to have their own engineering and steelwork department. This was to cut sub-contractor costs for the work which had to be contracted out in those fields. Having their own in house facilities would cut down on the expenditure. Thomas Mackenzie undertook the running and overseeing of the new department. After they were established the company started apprentices who were trained for five years until they were capable of dismantling, re-assembling and refitting any type of diesel engine and be able to install them in boats.

This rather grainy photograph is of the workforce at Herd & Mackenzie in 1919 - a vast increase from the workforce shown earlier at Findochty and reflects the rise in trade experienced after the First World War had run its course and the nation got back to a peace footing once more.

The new Herd & Mackenzie slipway was soon fully employed and because of its protected position and easy approach in any state of weather, became popular with skippers and owners over a wide area. At that time, the largest drifter fleet in the country was based in Buckie and District. The original yard at Findochty was still active and took its share of business along with the offspring at Buckie, but the latter easily outgrew the parent. The Findochty yard had produced 36 vessels mainly 85' steam drifters, three of which were 87' x 10' built as tenders and patrol vessels for the Admiralty. The only exception was Nautilus which was the first diesel boat for Findochty.

The slipway at Findochty and that at Buckie could only ever take one boat at a time, in order to rectify this at Buckie carriages and piers were built at both sides of the main slipway at Buckie. This proved to be a great benefit to the yard as up to four fishing vessels at a time could be accommodated on either side of the main slipway. The yard could slip and side slip Admiralty tank landing craft of 185 feet and 40 feet beam without any problem, as a whole the side slipping arrangements added greatly to the repairs section.

Mention must be made of the slipway steam winch which was made by Henderson's in Aberdeen and installed at Buckie in 1919. This winch gave yeoman service over the years having pulled up hundreds of boats of all types and never a hitch. It was finally dismantled when alterations were made to the slipway in 2005.

The First World War had another casualty that was not immediately evident during the turmoil but the arrival of the peace gave it new impetus to impact on the local economy. A major percentage of the herring caught by the fishermen of the Moray Coast ports had gone to the markets on the continent of Europe, with Russia and Germany being major buyers of the produce of the fishermen's skills. These markets had disappeared almost overnight when the war started and with Germany on its knees financially after the war, there was no market for fish and the whole industry went into a slump.

Russia, another huge consumer of herring, had gone through the Bolshevik revolution from 17th October 1917. This saw the end of Tsarist Russia and open markets. The Bolsheviks ran a 'workers state' and seized all the assets of the country for the people. The war years had seen a natural drop in herring catches, but the almost complete collapse of the markets pushed the whole industry into a slump. There was no point in catching fish without a market in which to sell the silver darlings. Fishing boats were laid up all over the country.

This had a knock-on effect in many of the industries who had a role to play in the fishing industry and, of course, affected the many boat builders including Herd & Mackenzie.

The 1920s and 1930s saw many of the boat building yards along the Moray Firth Coast from Wick to Fraserburgh experiencing real difficulties. Ten boatbuilding yards closed; only one yard survived and that was Herd & Mackenzie largely because they had their own slipway.   Herd & Mackenzie was also in the fortunate position of having a source of suitable boatbuilding timber in forests owned by Seafield Estates within a radius of 10 miles from the Yard. In order to reduce costs even further the employees had to fell, dress and then transport the timbers to the yard for processing.

Many of the skilled tradesmen had to leave the area in order find work. This leakage of skilled personnel would impact on future prosperity for the area as there would not be the same skills led base on which to build new jobs for the area. The same happens in the modern world where skilled craftsmen are laid off and have to re-locate to find work taking their valuable skills with them. The down side then and now is that many of the people with the skills did not return.

These were desperate times; skilled tradesmen had to do any type of menial work available. In many instances owners of fishing boats were employed using picks and shovels on the deepening of the inner basin of Buckie Harbour. Many herring fishermen went to Aberdeen to find work on the white-fish trawlers and a special train was laid on from Buckie as so many were travelling to and from Aberdeen.

Perfectly good fishing wooden fishing boats were changing hands for as little as £50.

Slowly conditions in the industry began to improve and Herd & Mackenzie was fortunate in receiving orders for a new type of fishing boat, mainly from fishermen in Lossiemouth.

At the end of 1924, Herd & Mackenzie won the first order for a new Steam Drifter for 10 years. This was for a wooden vessel with triple expansion steam engines from Lewis of Aberdeen. The firm built its last steam drifter in 1930 with the *Lizzie West* and *John Herd*. The last survivor, the *Lizzie West*, was broken up in 1968.

Some vessels were experimenting with seine-net fishing for white fish, a method of fishing evolved by the Danes. The Danes always had their boats painted a light blue colour, this was for eminently practical purposes, the local boats from Buckie and district went out every week for the week or less. By the time they got back to harbour the fish they had harvested was still reasonably fresh and in good condition. The Danes however went out for up to three weeks at a time and their fish holds could not cope with that length of time without risking the fish going off, one of the ideas they had was to reflect the sunlight back off their boats so that the inner holds stayed that bit cooler.

Other vessels were fitted as trawlers but in neither method of fishing were the Steam Drifters the ideal vessel, being too large and costly in operation for seining, and insufficient in power for legitimate trawling. Gradually the drifter trawlers went out of business, some reverting to herring fishing and others joining the ranks of the seine-net fleet. This fleet persisted until it became evident that a different type of vessel was essential. There was a demand for a smaller motor-driven vessel suitable for seine net fishing, and herring fishing in season.

In 1929, the firm built the motor-drifter *Nautilus* for Smith of Findochty. She was fitted with the first semi-diesel engine in the area and was a very successful craft. She was lost during the evacuation of troops from Dunkirk in 1940.

A number of vessels had been experimenting with seine-net fishing for white fish, this mode of fishing had been introduced at Grimsby in emulation of the Danish fishing fleet. Other vessels were fitted as trawlers but, in neither method of fishing was the steam drifter the ideal vessel, being too large and expensive for seine net fishing and not powerful enough for legitimate trawling.

Gradually the drifter-trawlers went out of business, some reverting to herring fishing and others joining the ranks of the seine net fleet. This fleet persisted until it became clearly evident that a different type of boat was essential.

Demand for the steam drifters fell away but the partners, as enterprising as ever, devoted their energies to the production of a smaller vessel, motor driven and suitable for seine net or herring fishing in season.

Guided by the experience of fishermen and their own building traditions they began a programme which carried on in the face of the lean years of the depression, had produced a sizeable fleet of motor boats by the time the Second World War broke out on 3rd September 1939.[5]

In 1932, the Fifie sterned motor boats, *Courage* and *Liberty*, followed for Findochty and Cullen owners. Between 1933 and 1939, twenty cruiser sterned seiners and seiner drifters, between 50 ft. and 65 ft. long, were built, mainly powered by 54, 68 or 72 h.p. Gardner diesel engines. Most of them were built for Lossiemouth, which was the pioneer seine-net port that in 1937 owned 81 boats.

The *Olive Leaf*, built in 1934 for the Thomson family of Lossiemouth, was powered by the first slow running full diesel engine, and the *Jeannie Mackay*, built for Helmsdale in 1938, was the first to be fitted with a high speed Gardner L3 type diesel engine, in the area.

With the outbreak of the Second World War in 1939, fishing vessels were rapidly fitted out for war service.

---

[5] Banffshire Advertiser 29th March 1956

> In this new emergency Herd & Mackenzie were immediately called upon to repeat its war programme of a previous generation. Fishing boats were rapidly fitted for war service while building to Admiralty order of various types of craft began and was carried out at increasing pace during the war.[6]

A number of 45 ft. and 75 ft M.F.V's (Motorised Fishing Vessels) and several 105 ft. and 126 ft. wooden motor minesweepers were built for the Admiralty to deal with both magnetic and acoustic mines. The yard built the first vessel to be equipped for sweeping acoustic mines.

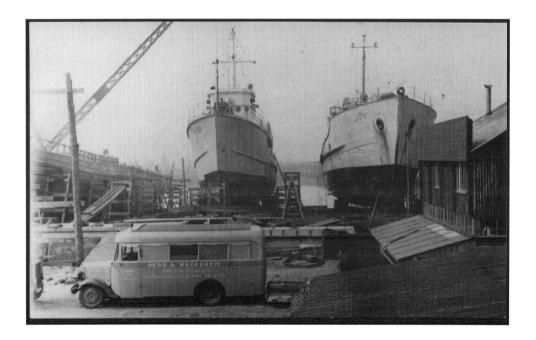

The Yard in Second World War mode

John Mackenzie recalls the visit by the Admiralty after they had completed the first minesweeper; it appeared that the Admiralty were in no rush to get the

---

[6] Banffshire Advertiser 29th March 1956

ship. He was shown a plan for the device that was to be installed on the front of the minesweeper.

"This was, in all respects a great bar swung across the forecastle head; an A frame swung from there right down over the stem and on the end of it there was a conical shaped steel bucket affair about 3 feet in diameter and 4 ½ feet long and 2 feet wide. When this bucket arrived, I was told, in no uncertain terms, that I could not allow anybody to look at what was inside that bucket. The Admiralty was insisting on that. I then asked the Admiralty how was anything to be coupled to it if you cannot get inside it. They did not have an answer. They eventually said OK. We put a tent over the whole thing on the pier and had a small crane on standby. We started to open it up very carefully indeed, we took off the cover and all that was there was a wee electrically operated Kangol hammer, this vibrated against the sides of the cone which was out in front of the ship and it was sending sound waves which would deal with the acoustic mines"

However, I learned that another more deadly mine had been developed by the Germans and one had been recovered in the Thames Estuary, a young man had gone out and taken it apart and it was found to be a magnetic mine. This caused another set of problems as to how to get a device that would sweep for these mines. We built skids that were tied together and a great heavy coil of copper wire that sent out a pulse was used to deal with the magnetic mines. Only problem was that they also blew up the skids and a method had to be found to combat that problem.

This was a very interesting story that John Mackenzie had related and further research revealed the following:-

 In the first couple of months of the Second World War came a new mine threat. Most contact mines leave holes in a ship's hulls, but some ships survived mine blasts, limping back to port with buckled plates, popped rivets, and broken backs. This latest threat appeared to be due to a new type of magnetic mine, detonating at a distance from the ships, and doing the damage with the shockwave of the explosion.

Often ships that had successfully run the gauntlet of the Atlantic crossing were destroyed entering freshly mineswept harbors on Britain's coast. More shipping was now being lost than could be replaced, and Churchill ordered that the intact recovery of one of these new mines was to be given highest priority.

In 1939 a Grimsby fisherman, Wally Hayes, volunteered to go out and find one and bring it back intact. He was the skipper of the 'Ray of Hope' and he was keen to do his bit for King and Country. His bravery was undoubted as he sailed off into the minefields in search of an magnetic mine. He found one and actually passed over it which had the effect of detonating it. Wally Hayes was blown through the roof of his bridge and was only one of two survivors of the crew of the Ray of Hope. He was awarded the Distinguished Service Cross in January 1940 for his deeds.

Then the British experienced a stroke of luck in November 1939. A German mine was dropped from an aircraft laying mines onto the mud flats of the Thames Estuary, well above the waterline. As if this was not sufficiently good fortune, the land happened to belong to the army, and a base, including men and workshops, was close at hand. The rendering safe and recovery of the first German magnetic mine (Type GA) at Shoeburyness on 24 November 1939.

The magnetic mine recovered at Shoeburyness

They had an idea that the mines used magnetic sensors, everyone removed all metal, including buttons, made new tools out of non-magnetic brass. They disarmed the mine and rushed it to labs at Portsmouth.   For this deed, Commander John Ouvry R.N. was decorated with the DSO by King George VI.

The magnetic mine recovery team with Cdr Ouvry on the right with his back to the camera

It was now up to the scientists who discovered a new type of arming mechanism inside. The arming mechanism had a sensitivity level that could be set, the units of the scale were in milligauss. Gauss is a measurement for the strength of a magnetic field, demonstrating how it went off before coming into contact with the ship.

Using the detector from the mine, they were able to study the effect of a ship passing near it. A ship or any large ferrous object passing through the earth's magnetic field will concentrate the field at that point. The detector from the mine, sensitive to this effect, was designed to go off at the mid-point of the ship passing overhead.

From this crucial data, methods were developed to clear the mines. Early methods included the use of large electromagnets dragged behind ships.

However this method had the disadvantage of "sweeping" only a small strip at a time.

A better solution was found in the form of electrical cables dragged behind ships, passing a large current through the seawater. This induced a huge magnetic field and swept the entire area between the two ships.

Although the Motor Minesweepers lacked the power to tow sweeps for contact mines they were suitable for handling equipment for combating magnetic mines and some later models were fitted with an acoustic hammer on an retractable "A" frame over the bows for countering acoustic mines.

So history shows that the Herd & Mackenzie yard at Buckie had a big part to play in the successful countermeasures against both acoustic mines and magnetic mines.

Another wartime scene from the Yard showing Minesweepers on the slipway

The Second World War ended and the country had to get back to a commercial footing once again. The death toll of experienced skippers and seamen from the Buckie area was again very heavy.

The end of the war signalled another busy time with the reconversion of vessels commandeered by the Admiralty being re-rigged for peacetime use. There was also a pent-up demand for new fishing vessels.

Between 1946 and 1950 Twenty-three seiners and seine drifters up to 75 ft long, with 20 ft. beam were completed. These were a little larger and more robust than pre-war vessels, and with more powerful engines to give a greater sea range and carrying capacity. They were partly financed with grants and loans from the Herring Industry Board and the Scottish Home Department. Fourteen were powered by Gardner L3 engines of 114 or 152 h.p. with 6 or 8 cylinders. The majority had Lossiemouth winches and Beccles coilers. By 1950, the demand for new fishing vessels had been met and it became difficult to obtain new orders.

When the steam drifters returned from the Yarmouth fishing in November most were laid-up for the winter. This gave the yard time to do all the necessary repairs before the summer fishing. It was then all go. The boat owners would come and place an order for his boat to be cleaned and painted from keel to top of mast, casing grained and names gilded. The painters were kept busy. Graining of casings became a competition between all the 'grainers' in the port as to who was best and the man who always come out top was Willie Murray 'Gyke' who was the foreman painter in the yard. He could make a cold steel casing look as if it was made of growing wood panels.

There never was a more beautiful fleet of drifters than that which sailed out of Buckie Harbour at the start of the summer fishing.

During the 1950 boat-building slump, orders were obtained for 152 ft. and 105 ft. composite aluminium alloy and wood minesweepers as part of the Admiralty's rearmament programme in the face of the 'Cold War'. An aircraft hangar was acquired and put up on the west side of the slipway at Buckie to enable minesweepers up to a length of 152 ft. to be constructed under cover. Between 1950 and 1960, four coastal, 152ft minesweepers and two inshore minesweepers, 105 ft. long were built for the Royal Navy.

Willie Stewart and George Sutherland two of the highly skilled French Polishers employed at the Yard
They were employed on the woodwork for the officer's mess and cabins on the minesweepers built.

In 1951 both founders of the firm died, 48 years after they founded the enterprise, and Mr Mackenzie's son, John became managing partner.

Ill-health and the years of hard work and worry had taken their toll, however, and the partners died in 1951 within months of each other, leaving behind them a worthy monument to their sterling character and fine craftsmanship.[7]

In the early 1950s, land was acquired on the south side of Commercial Road, opposite the slipway. A large building was erected, housing the metal fabrication shop for the manufacture of deckhouses, whalebacks and components for hulls in steel and aluminium. A sawmill for working all the timber required for wood construction was also built. Workshops for the joiners, engineers, painter and the stores were in the main yard.

---

[7] Banffshire Advertiser 29th March 1956

Following the initiation, on 11th August 1953, of the White Fish Authority's grant and loan scheme, and with prospects of much Admiralty work, Herd and Mackenzie took over boat building premises at Greenhill, Peterhead. These premises formerly belonged to George Forbes & Co. and situated on the Island of Keith Inch. During the busy period covered by the minesweeper programme, employment built up to 250 at Buckie and 45 at Peterhead.

WJ Carter, P Fraser, J Scott and W Murray together in 1953 each of them had 30 years service.

John Mackenzie recalls that when he went down to see the yard he did not have one workman for the place, all had left the town following the closure of the various yards and had settled in many places throughout the country. He went down to the Department of Employment offices in the town and asked if they had any carpenters on their books as he required a number of them to help build boats. The short answer from the clerk was that there was none looking for work, except perhaps one man, a 72 years old retired carpenter who was still keen to carry on with his trade.

The Peterhead work force 1954 with the trawler Vigilance A126 behind them.

Back row L-R:
Stan Cowie, Gilbert Rankin, John Reid, Jim Duncan, Danny Gordon, John Hay,
NK Davidson
Middle row L-R:
Andy Cordiner, NK, Tom West, Alex J. Stephen, Buller Martin, John Buchan,
NK Lamb, NK,
Front Row L-R:
Hector Reid, NK, William Buchan, Jack Allardyce, William Pert, Jim Buchan
(Sunshine), NK, Jackie McLean, NK, Stanley Walker, NK , George L. Cordiner,
David Hill, NK ,
John Clark (Manager) John Buchan (Foreman), NK.-

From 1954 to 1965, sixty-five fishing boats were built to various designs at
Buckie and Peterhead. These included Scottish Type seiners and seiner trawlers
up to 75 ft. long, Danish type seiners for England, a Canadian type gill-net boat,
and in 1958 a large 109 ft. long, 23 ft. beam wooden trawler, the **Vigilance**.
Eleven yachts from 65 ft. long down to 30 ft. long were also built in wood during
this period. There were two overseas orders, an 89 ft. cargo passenger vessel for
the British Solomon Islands, and a 67 ft. Fishery Research Vessel for Aden. In
1964, the Peterhead yard was closed and building concentrated at Buckie.

In 1955, another stage in the development was reached with the first steel, I00 ft. line-fisher, the **Loch Kildonan,** for W Stewart and others, which was laid down at Buckie. A steel trawler, 130 ft. long, the **Star of Loretto**, followed in 1956, and delivered to the Walker Steam Trawl Company of Aberdeen in 1958.

The launch of the Loch Kildonan

In his constant search for new business and new ideas John Mackenzie was in the United States and Canada during 1955. While visiting Vancouver in British Columbia he met a man by the name of James Flett and his wife. James Flett had been a native of Findochty and had left the village when he was 17 years old to seek a new life in Vancouver. Mr Flett was 74 years of age in 1955.

When John Mackenzie visited their home he was able to tell Jim Flett that Herd & Mackenzie had built the Petrel for his cousin in Findochty. Mrs Flett then said she had a photograph of the boat and she began to search a large bundle of photographs to show it to their guest. Then John spotted a photograph that he thought he recognised. This photograph had been like the Holy Grail to John Mackenzie as he recognised the first boat ever built by Herd & Mackenzie in 1905, the Bloomfield. This was the boat that the whole history of the company had started with and he had been trying to get a copy of a photograph of it ever since he knew of it. His search, thus far, had been in vain until now and here he was 'as far away as ye could get almost' in Vancouver with the photograph in his hand.

He obtained a copy of the black and white photograph and took it home, he sent it to a photographic company in London in the hope that they could enhance the copy but it was a black and white photograph and that was it.

One day he was speaking to his friend Captain John Hourie from Orkney, who owned the Orkney Islands Trading Company, who told him of an artist by the name of Harry Berry who lived on the Islands and was a artist of great standing there. He did all of the Royal National Lifeboat Institution boat paintings and was very highly thought of. John Mackenzie asked his friend Captain Hourie if he would ask Mr Berry to paint a likeness of his black and white photograph in colour. The painting was eventually completed and delivered to John Mackenzie.

The black and white photograph of the beginning at Findochty

The same scene after Harry Berry had finished.

The artist had utilised all his talents in painting what he thought the scene would look like in living colour. It has to be said that he made a wonderful job of the project and produced a painting that typifies the pioneering ship building that was taking place on a piece of rugged coast line in the Moray Firth by skilled craftsmen who were proud of their work.

Captain Hourie delivered the painting to John Mackenzie but there was also a letter written by the artist Harry Berry included when Captain Hourie picked up the finished painting. The content of the letter tells its own story as to how the artist had seen his finished work and how he had been in awe of the skills of the men who built the boats.

The letter reads;-

Seaview,
Melsetter
June 14th

Dear Captain Hourie

Herewith the painting and I hope you like it. If you had <u>described</u> the photo, without my seeing it, and then asked me if I would paint it , I would probably have said NO, especially after painting the Lifeboats with their theme of sea-violence v seamanship; your old photograph would have sounded a very boring subject, but as soon as I saw it, I could see a great story, for it at once spoke of a rare moment in the history of Scottish shipbuilding that has gone forever, of ships built under primitive conditions by men who were truly shipwrights, worthy fellows with calloused hands, who gave an honest days work – and took a personal pride in doing that work. A way of life that has gone. For them a ship was 'built', not assembled; the tenon and mortise, the steaming and careful fitting, chip by chip, each piece a work of time and care, where the crude crosscut and ripsaw, the axe and the adze were precise tools in the hands of men who knew how to use them. Perhaps they didn't build classy ships – but they built good ones, sound, first class ships for first class seamen to sail in.

I noticed too, the half built ship with a fresh coat of paint – the gingerbread of the headboard guilded, as if her builder could not wait, but must see his half grown lily adorned. He would have been proud, and rightly so, for it was the humble beginnings such as these that came to make 'Scottish Built' the Hall-Mark of quality where ships were concerned. A pity this breed has gone, and much of their know-how with them, buried under a welter of power packed machinery, gadget filled workshops, prefabricated and component parts, and replaced by a newer breed of technicians clamouring for their official   tea-breaks and shorter hours, where a ship is not a thing of beauty into which they can build something of 'themselves', but rather a necessary evil that must be dealt with dispassionately. I may be old fashioned, but to me, even ships have lost their individuality!

I saw all this, and much more in the old photo, so I painted it.

If Mr Mackenzie likes the picture, I would like to (price) for it – if he doesn't like it, then he need not of course pay for it. I will understand, for I would not pay for anything I did not want either. In any case, I shall have been well rewarded for in painting it, it has given me many pleasant (and sad) meditations that all the guineas in the world could not buy.

Kind regards
Yours
Signed Harry B

The letter from Harry Berry to Captain Hourie meant much to John H Mackenzie as it was obvious that the artist had managed to see what lay behind the stark outline of three boats on a rocky shore. He saw beyond the bits of wood, to the skills and demeanour of the men who had built the boats with a great pride in their craft.

Hector Stronach at work in the Engineering workshop

In 1958 the word 'demarcation' was one that spread like a cancer as it made the rounds of the boat and ship yards of Scotland. The trades jealously guarded 'their' work. No one else was allowed to do even the smallest job if there was a tradesman employed by the company whose job it was to do that particular job. While in some instances, it could be said that this was a good thing as it meant that only men trained to whatever level he was skilled, would do the job for which he had been trained, some other person who did not hold the skills of the particular tradesman involved would not do it.   However, after time, many thought that demarcation became more and more ridiculous with simple jobs taking a group of men to get the job done.

All this waiting around for a particular tradesman to perhaps drill a hole before a screw could be inserted was time consuming and expensive, with highly skilled tradesmen hanging around waiting for their turn to do their bit of the job.

It arrived at the Herd & Mackenzie yard one day when a representative of one group of tradesmen came to John Mackenzie's office and demanded a raise in wages or the whole of the group of tradesmen concerned would be out on strike on Monday following. The representative had only been with the company for a week and had moved to the yard from one of the Aberdeen Yards where they were making more money on piecework. The men in Herd & Mackenzie Yard were more flexible and could turn their hand to any small job that required few skills to complete. They were being paid less than their counterparts in Aberdeen where demarcation was a way of life but was slowly strangling the industry.

The upshot of the visit was the man leaving with a flea in his ear from the Managing Director to carry out his threat and see what would happen. The men in the steelwork and welding sections walked out in support of the claim – the remainder of the work force had nothing to do with the strike and stayed to continue working. It was inevitable that the demarcation disputes affecting the whole industry would show up at Buckie at some time or other. It had arrived and would be dealt with as fairly and as diplomatically as possible.

John Mackenzie did not show it or say it, but he was genuinely disappointed and quite devastated. He truly thought his men were more sensible and would see through the whole shambles that demarcation in such a small yard would bring, and that they would back him. For once in his life, he got it wrong.

His father and uncles had started a firm that from the first day looked after the workers at the yard. It was like joining a family and worked under that concept for many years in friendly paternalism. The management had prided themselves that they provided work for upwards of about 250 men (and more) and all from a radius of 10 miles for so from Buckie.

The strike went on and on for twelve long weeks before the striking workers returned. They had lost three months wages and not gained a penny on their wages when they returned. In addition, their action had destroyed any remaining modicum of paternalism within the yard. John Mackenzie addressed the workers before they returned to work on their return and left them in no doubt that their position and that of their other work colleagues had changed. From that moment on they would be paid employees getting their full entitlement under the laws of the land. A way of life in the yard had gone forever.

Without getting into the politics of it all, bystanders, who know little of the way of life of a company must wonder, why, when they had a management that listened to their grievances and paid what was regarded as a fair days pay for a fair days work, did they really want to lose that relationship with their employer?

It may be that the more cynical in the workforce thought that little would change, they would be wrong in thinking that way, as from then on it was a case of "I am the boss and you are my employees". Many critics of paternalistic owners of companies had some justification in rebelling against the way companies were being run, but common sense had to play a part too and that was not always part of the thinking when such action was being considered.

The strike pushed through more changes than were evident at first sight.

In 1959 a new company, Herd & Mackenzie Ltd. was formed and took over the assets of the business from the partners. John Herd Mackenzie was appointed as Chairman and Managing Director and John Herd, son of James Herd became the Secretary. The other directors were Mrs Martha Herd and Mrs Mary Ann Mackenzie.

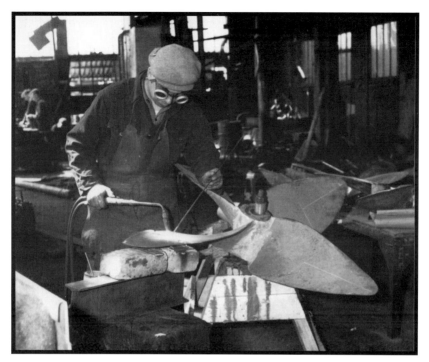

Bill Seath working on a propeller in the Engineering workshop

From 1966 to 1976, thirty-nine vessels, three in steel, were built, and four yachts.

The most notable vessel completed was the 144ft. sail trainer schooner, **Captain Scott** in 1971, in wood for the Dulverton Trust. This was the largest sailing vessel completed in the UK since the Second World War.

On 1st March 1968, a director's meeting was convened and it was noted that the Companies Act 1967 required all companies, both private and public, to file copies of annual accounts with the registrar of Companies. In order to avoid doing this it was resolved that the company should be re-incorporated as an unlimited company.

In 1979 on the retirement of John Herd Mackenzie, the ownership of the Yard passed to the Fisherman's Mutual Association (Buckie) Ltd.

There can be little doubt in anyone's mind that the yard had been kept going by the drive and personality of John Mackenzie for the thirty years he had control of the yard. He worked tirelessly to ensure that the yard always had an order on their books. He was the sales division, the marketing division, the human resources division, the decision maker.

He did more jobs himself than was really good for him but he kept the yard going along with his trusted lieutenants and his work force of whom he was really proud, no matter the minor past difficulties.

So that was the end of family connection with Herd & Mackenzie but the name lived on for a number of years under the Fishermen's Mutual Association and then under a Management Buy Out team before finally being sold to Jones Shipyard in the 1990s. That was the end of the line for the Herd & Mackenzie name as it was quickly dispensed with by the Jones management.

The yard still exists under the Lithgow Group of companies of which Jim Farquhar has a connection. It is now called the Buckie Shipyard and is still employing a good number of men from the town.

Recollections of working in the Herd & Mackenzie Yard

To add to the story of the yard it was considered appropriate to interview a small number of people who worked in the yard over the years to ask for their recollections of their time working in the Herd & Mackenzie yard.

Jim Farquhar

Jim Farquhar was a local boy who left Buckie High School aged 15 in the spring of 1954. His mind was set as to what he wanted to do and that was to be a painter in the shipyard. His grandfather William Murray 'Bealy Gyke' worked at the shipyard and was not keen for his grandson to join him in the yard. However, he never stood in his way as it was obvious that young Jim was determined to become a painter in the local shipyard and nothing was going to stop him.

He attended at the yard and was interviewed by Jimmy Carter the Yard Manager. Jimmy Carter was a good friend of John Mackenzie; indeed, it was he who had handed over the keys of his motorbike to his friend many years before. That was followed by the accident that left John Mackenzie with a badly mangled leg that never recovered really and left him with one leg shorter than the other and a permanent limp.

Jimmy Carter was an engineer to trade and asked the young Farquhar if he would not rather be an engineer in the yard or even a carpenter. The reply was that he wanted to be a painter. Nothing could shift him apparently and so he got the job as a painter's apprentice starting on 5th April 1954.

The young Jim Farquhar worked under four journeymen painters, Simon Clark who specialised in painting the names and numbers on the boats. Sandy Muir who specialised in what was known as 'graining' which was painting imitation grain on wood or steel. Walter Reid who specialised in Lifeboats and had an excellent 'brush hand' – i.e. he was good with a paintbrush. Lastly, Jimmy Whyte was another specialist in the art of 'Graining'.

These four journeymen worked under their foreman who was William Murray the maternal grandfather of young Jim. He in turn reported to Jimmy Carter. They ensured that Jim's education in painting covered all skills and aspects of the job, his grandfather wanted him to obtain the necessary skills in each and every job in the painting trade within the yard.

Jim left the yard in 1960 to complete his National Service in the Royal Air Force.

In 1959 his grandfather retired and was replaced as foreman by Simon Clark, he was foreman for four years before he too retired in 1963. Jim Farquhar was promoted to foreman painter in succession to Simon Clark by the yard manager Jimmy Carter. Jimmy Carter died just afterwards, a relatively young man in his 50s.

John Clark was appointed yard manager at Buckie. He had been the manager running the yard at Peterhead which he had built up from a couple of bare areas into a thriving yard. One of his greatest achievements whilst at the yard was the building and launching of a 105 ft wooden trawler the Vigilance, all the work on that had been done with the bare minimum of crane and lifting facilities. This meant that the heavy oak timbers used in the construction had to be manhandled. It was a tribute to his skills and to the determination of the workforce that the job was completed on time. John Clark managed the yard until it completed its last order in 1964 and closed.

A few years later John Clark, who was a shipwright/carpenter to trade, was appointed joint General Manager of the yard at Buckie with Bill Farquhar. Bill was a draughtsman working in the drawing office and he was responsible for all office work in the yard including estimating the costing for new vessels and repairs. A further manager was Bill Allison who was manager in charge of building Minesweepers and other specialist projects until he retired when he was in his seventies.

The clear lines of responsibility were thus drawn up for the future life of the yard with an internal manager and a yard manager responsible for all of the work and reporting direct to John Mackenzie.

By 1976 John Clark was approaching retirement age and John Mackenzie appointed Jim Farquhar as an assistant to John Clark with a view to learning the running of the yard from John Clark and to step into his job once he had retired. At the end of 1977 Jim Farquhar was appointed Joint General Manager with Bill Farquhar, John Clark remained in his position with a gradual shift in the decision-making process as he approached his retirement.

John Mackenzie retired and in 1979 the Yard was sold to the Fishermans Mutual Association (F.M.A.), a group of fishermen who operated a sort of Co-operative type organisation with all the parts of the fishing and building being taken under control.

A number of changes were made in the yard; Bill Farquhar left the yard and took up a directorship at Macduff where he remains to this day. A General Manager was appointed, Bill Neale, he was from Northumberland. Jim Farquhar remained as yard manager. Bill Neale was only there a short time before he left and returned to England.

In 1982 the Queen was visiting the North East of Scotland and during her time she visited Buckie where Jones Shipyard and the Herd & Mackenzie shipyard were both on her agenda. She also visited the Fishermen Memorial Chapel in New Street Buckie before departing for Baxter's in Fochabers and then to Elgin.

Jim Farquhar was given the pleasant task of showing the Royal party round the Herd & Mackenzie yard. The Queen was very gracious and very knowledgeable about ship building in general and asked many questions. The Duke of Edinburgh having been an officer in the Royal Navy was well acquainted with the various tasks involved in ship-building.

The Queen visits the yard 1982 and is shown round by Jim Farquhar

In 1985 the F.M.A. went into receivership, the yard was retained by the receiver and sold to a Management Buy Out (M.B.O.) later in 1985.

Jim Farquhar was part of the MBO team which had 4 directors beside him namely Iain Sinclair, Eric Smith and Edward Acton, the fourth director was a representative of the Investment In Industry (3I group).

The yard had been saved and no one had lost their job which was one of the main objectives of the MBO.

In 1992 the company, with the active directors nearing retirement age and no secured future for the company, was sold as a going concern to Jones Shipyard. There had been considerable but friendly rivalry between the yards for many years but if one or other needed any assistance then it would be given without questions.

Sadly the name of Herd & Mackenzie vanished from that moment on as Jones name was preferred for both yards.

A number of redundancies were made where duplication was evident but the majority of the work-force remained in employment.

John Mackenzie had remained in touch with Jim Farquhar since he his retired at the end of the seventies and was always interested in what was going on in the yard and how the whole works was progressing.

It would be remiss not to mention the Royal National Lifeboat Institution (RNLI) who have been a client of Herd & Mackenzie since the 1930s and who have loyally maintained the contract and connection with the Buckie yard over the period. The RNLI is a highly respected part of the communities along the Moray Coast and indeed, throughout the UK for the valuable services it provides.

The yard is still in existence under the umbrella of The Lithgow Group. It has seen many changes over the years most of which have been positive. The yard updated its facility for dealing with the Lifeboats by erecting a new shed in 2002 incorporating a heated paint cell capable of accommodating the largest vessel in the RNLI fleet. In conjunction a new slipway was built on the south side of the yard and a 50 ton travel hoist which transports the boats from the inner basin of the harbour to the new facility. Since these improvements, the RNLI work scope has increased.

Jim Farquhar is still a part of the yard after fully 53 years and is now a non-executive director who works on a part time basis as required.

When the idea of this book was first mooted it was to Jim Farquhar that the team turned to with his intimate knowledge of events that had happened in the yard in times past. He organised the meetings with John Mackenzie, provided the expertise and was able to put names to faces in the many pictures that were made available.

With the passing of John Mackenzie, who was to write the foreword, it was an easy decision to make to ask Jim to write the foreword. After all he said that John Mackenzie always called him 'ma loon' and who better could write the words his old friend and mentor would have written.

Recollections from

William 'Bill' Cowie

I served my time as an engineer with John Duncan & Co, I started with them in 1937 and was there for 11 years before the firm went out of business in July 1948. I spent most of my time at Duncan's servicing boats which had been in the war, mostly work from the Admiralty during the war years and carrying out repairs to fishing boats which were still going through the war years.

All the work was on small boats, we had some High Speed boats from the Admiralty which were similar to MTB's taking out the machinery, servicing it and then replacing it back in the boats. All the underwater slip work was done at Jones yard.

Of course during the war we had the 'Shetland Bus' which was the Free Norwegians who had fled their country following the invasion by the Germans during 1941. Many of them fled to the UK in fishing boats and headed for the Shetland Isles where they set up a sort of refugee reception place. They then began to fight a guerrilla war from there and other places to try and fight back against the Germans who were in their country.

Many came to Buckie and worked with us in looking after the boats which went back and forth between Scotland and Norway to provide support for the underground movement in Norway and to infiltrate agents into the country by boat.

There were a lot of people from Norway in the area during the war, a young couple lived down the street from here (his home in Ianstown) and they fitted in without a problem, their children soon became fluent in both languages. Some married local girls or local boys and they were made very welcome.

In August 1948 I went to try and get a job at Herd & Mackenzie's yard, I went along with Gilbert Smith who had served his apprenticeship alongside me in Duncan's. We went and knocked on the office window and it opened and a girl asked us what we wanted, I asked if it was possible if we could see Mr Carter (yard Manager) or Mr John Mackenzie (the boss) about a job. She shut the window saying that they would be in the yard and to go and seek them out. Gilbert turned to me and remarked that 'it doesn't look very promising'. Little did I know then that not only would I get a job but I would also marry the girl in the office.

John Mackenzie told us both that many of the fishing boats were being prepared for the Yarmouth fishing and that there was plenty of work to do, he could hire us for three weeks but after that it depended on the amount of work there was about the yard. Those 3 weeks stretched into 34 years and I loved just about every minute of my work with Herd & Mackenzie, I had absolutely no regrets whatsoever.

John Mackenzie gave his men a free hand, he would listen to your opinion but he was always the boss. No one could pull the wool over his eyes; he was a fair man to work for although we had the occasional disagreement

There was always a rule in the yard that the slip had priority over everything, what this meant is that any boat on the slip awaiting to go in the water had top priority in getting attention for whatever it needed because it was critical that it caught the tide.

One day John Mackenzie came into the machine shop and said to me that he needed something done urgently for one of his private boats, I replied that I already had an urgent job to do as I was machining a part for the boat on the slip and that took priority so his job would have to wait. He turned and said " Trying to get an urgent job done here is almost impossible, I will have to get Hamilton's

(A local engineering company) to do the work for me as no one here will do it". Mind he was laughing at the time.

I was a skilled journeyman and my wages at the time were £4.19.11d take home pay - that was for a forty seven hour week, these days that princely sum is equivalent to £4.99p. It was always my wish to get my wages up to £10 a week; I thought that would make me happy once I achieved that.

In 1950 the yard won a contract from the Admiralty to build inshore and coastal minesweepers. Just after we heard I was called into Mr Mackenzie's office and he told me about the contract and asked me to take charge of providing the machine parts required for the new contract. I was made a foreman with Gilbert Smith also promoted to foreman, he had responsibility for the machine shop repair work for the fishing boats, the boats needed an overhaul once a year and ever couple of years the engine needed to come out and be taken apart and rebuilt with new parts as required.

We worked well together and ran the machine shop satisfactorily, we manufactured many of the parts we needed, if they could not be bought in we made them ourselves on the equipment we had in the shop.

Bill Cowie working on the Aureola's rudder stalk on a centre lathe

At that time we were also building steel trawlers for Aberdeen and I was responsible for the machinery installation on them as well as on the Minesweepers. We built 2 inshore Minesweepers and 4 Coastal Minesweepers over the next ten years.

In 1965 Gilbert Smith left the company to become a marine surveyor for a Boat insurance company, his right hand man Jimmy Grant took over as foreman in his place. The team in the machine shop were all good men, by that time we could turn our hand to making just about everything on the shop floor as the expertise of the men was built upon over the years. John Mackenzie often said – "if we cannae buy it we can make it"

L to R Alex Matthews Foreman Plater, Jimmy Grant Foreman Engineer, John Clark Yard Manager, Billy Cowie Machine Shop Foreman, Joe Sutherland Foreman Joiner

John Mackenzie retired and the place was never the same without him around, it would never really be the same again, he was a complete one off, he was just like yon Richard Whiteley on Countdown, nothing was the same after he left and so it was with John Mackenzie. I was very happy during my time at Herd & Mackenzie and I would do it all again.

My wife and I decided to take early retirement in 1982, she had been with the company longer than I had but it was time to go for both of us. We have very fond memories of our time at the yard and with our colleagues there.

Recollections
Eunice Cowie (Gardiner)

I started work in 1940 with the Clydesdale bank in Findochty; I lived with my parents in Cullen at the time. I worked there for about three years before I took up a position in the office at Herd & Mackenzie. The Second World War was in full swing and I shifted to a job of work of National Importance, Herd & Mackenzie used to bank with the Clydesdale in Findochty.

When I was 21 years of age I was made cashier. I was responsible for the time sheets of the men; each of the men in the yard would have a unique number. I soon knew their individual numbers better than I knew their names.

For calculating the wages the week started from Wednesday and finished on a Tuesday, all the men's time sheets were to be in the office by Wednesday morning. All that day the time sheets had to be converted by calculating the amount of wages each individual would get for the hours he worked. Once that was completed a telephone call would be made to the bank in Findochty to tell them how much we would need for wages for the week and in what denominations, notes, silver and copper.

On the Friday morning me and Mr Mackenzie would go together to the bank for the money and once back in the office it would be checked, each individual's wages would be put in a wage packet ready for the men.

The men would line up outside in numerical order in the afternoon to get their wage packet at the office window, they would shout out their number and I would check I had given them the right wage packet and that was the routine that was worked every week.

I used to do all my calculations with a pencil and paper, I was not comfortable using the calculators that were starting to show up in the office. I always had another person working with me, young lassies mostly but they came and went regularly.

I would try and use the calculating machines but I never did trust them, a wrong button pushed would mean a mistake and that would not do at all. I preferred to use the old fashioned way. Mr Mackenzie came into the office one day when I was trying to get to grips with a calculating machine and he said, "I never thought I would live to see the day I would see you at a machine".

He was right; I was just not comfortable with the new technology, much preferring the pencil and paper method. In 1982 I retired from the company along with my husband, we had both had a wonderful time at Herd & Mackenzie, it was work but it was an enjoyable place to work, you felt as though you were part of a team that all worked together for each other and that was nice.

It would be difficult to include everyone who ever worked in the company in this book, however some are worthy of special mention because of their service to the company. It was to them and people like them who were much respected within the company that build up the company that gained respect from the industry. They were the backbone of the company as John Mackenzie said on more than one occasions during the visits to his home in December 2006. He had tremendous respect for the workforce and that shone through as he spoke in such glowing terms of 'his people'.

Jean Flett

Jean Flett started work in the Yard at the same time as Jim Farquhar, she as a junior clerkess and Jim as an apprentice painter. Jean worked in the accounts department and by the time she had finished working was the Head of accounts. She gave 45 years of sterling service and one remarkable fact about that was that she did not have one day off because of sickness during her entire service with Herd & Mackenzie and the companies who took over after John Mackenzie retired.

The office staff L to R

Andrea Spence, Gwen Rumbles, Jean Flett, Sheila Donald, Eunice Cowie, Alison Findlay

Jimmy Grant

It would also be remiss to fail to acknowledge the contribution made to the history of the yard without a mention of James George Grant known as Jimmy or Dodie.

Jimmy Grant started at Herd & Mackenzie on 5th November 1940 as an apprentice engineer working alongside John H. Mackenzie and under Jimmy Carter. After his apprenticeship was completed Jimmy continued his learning, he gleaned information from many sources as he built up his considerable skills base.

He was given more and more responsibility for the installation of the machinery in the new vessels. During the 1950s- 1970s he was responsible for installing the majority of engines in fishing vessels.

On the retiral of Gilbert Smith he was promoted to foreman and along with Billy Cowie ran the engineering division. On Billy's subsequent retirement Jimmy Grant assumed overall control and responsibility for the engineers.

His reputation as a first class engineer was reinforced by the esteem in which he was held by many fishing boat skippers. He was very approachable and with his intimate knowledge of the mechanics of fishing boat engines he was always available to hand out advice to anyone who asked. With the introduction of hydraulic systems on fishing boats he made it his top priority to gain as much knowledge as he could muster on the subject.

That was his way, he started learning as apprentice on his first day and was modest enough to admit that he was still learning when he completed over 50 years service at the yard

Jimmy Grant retired on 10th September 1991 and this highly respected engineer passed away on 6th February 2002.

Presentation by Jimmy Grant on the right to Billy & Eunice Cowie on their retirement in June 1982

Recollections

Joseph Sutherland
A.K.A. Joe the Joiner

Born in Findochty in 1924 – now aged 82.

I left school at age 14 years in 1938 and went straight to work for a local baker, Mackenzie, who came from Dingwall. I worked on the van with Mr Mackenzie who suffered a rupture and was unable to jump up and down out of the van so he had me as his boy, running up to the doors and selling bread.

I am related to the owners of one of the boats built by Herd & Mackenzie in the early days, the Smith brothers of Findochty who ordered the Nautilus. The skipper's son Alex and I used to go for a walk together for a yarn and he told me the following story. The background to this is the timing, as it took place in the days of the late nineteen twenties, early thirties, when many yards were struggling to make ends meet with extremely few orders being made by fishermen who were themselves struggling to cope with crippling debts.

James Herd had been in the Smith's house in Findochty after he heard that the brothers were thinking of a new boat, he said to them that it was important for Herd & Mackenzie to win the order as they were in similar straits as the other shipbuilders in the area and there was a distinct danger that Herd & Mackenzie may have to close their yard because of lack of business.

The Smith brothers decided to place their order with Herd & Mackenzie and this order arrived in 1929 to build the Nautilus, the boat was completed in 1930, it was fitted with the 'new' diesel engines that were just coming in at that time, it was called a semi-diesel, I think it was because it needed a set of blow lamps on the top of it, blowing heat onto a metal ball shaped object that sat on top of the engine, this cylinder was heated by the torches to make the engine run.

Just after the war started the Nautilus was commandeered by the Admiralty for war duties, she was down at Dunkirk assisting with the evacuation of troops from the temporary piers on the beaches. Having loaded herself full of soldiers she slipped her moorings and was immediately attacked by a bomber who dropped bombs on either side of the Boat. She was lifted up in the air in the explosions and when back in the water immediately began to leak in a number of places as the hull had been breached. The skipper got her to the destroyer and managed to get all the troops off and the crew before abandoning the sinking Nautilus.

In 1939 I went to sea on the Drifter Laurel Bank as a cook for the summer fishing. Wick to Thurso, through the Pentland Firth and then back down to Shields in Northumberland. On our way back home we had to stop in at Berwick to get bread as we had run out. When we arrived at Peterhead it was obvious that the whole of fishing fleet were in harbour, it was very strange and we did not know why that should be. The skipper had said to us he had never seen the like before; there were huge shoals of herring out at sea off Peterhead and not a local boat in sight. We shot our nets and drifted as night fell. The next thing I knew I was being wakened up in the night and told to put on a life jacket and stand out of the deck for safety, not to go below. I could hear the whooping of destroyers and could make out a huge fleet of warships passing through the area where we were fishing. Unknown to us, as no one had a radio in any of the boats we were with, Mr Churchill had ordered the Home fleet to its wartime quarters at Scapa Flow and they had steamed up that day after a review at Portsmouth. The start of the war was still a month away as it was only August but the First Sea Lord (Churchill) wanted to be sure his fleet were not caught napping. We were in their path; thankfully we survived without incident as did the rest of our small group of boats. We returned home with a hold full of herring.

A young Joe Sutherland can be seen on the right of both photographs – others featuring are John Hugh Anderson with the pipe in both photographs and a lad -In the left photo an William John Smith with the dog in the second photograph.

In the 1930s many of the shipwrights were out of work in the yards up and down the Moray coast and a lot of them from the area went down to Manchester where they were employed by aircraft manufacturer Fairey.
They moved their families south where they were earning good money in this relatively new industry.

The war started and the Ministry of War ordered them back to the Buckie area so they could aid the war effort by building and repairing boats. A lot of them were not happy about this as it meant uprooting their families from their homes and schools in Manchester and heading north once again. One of the common phrases at the time "There is a war on" was answer enough to most of their questions. The effort would need every man and woman in the country pulling their weight to enable to keep the country going during the war.

When I got back home from my summer fishing trip, I worked for the bakers again for a few months before I got an apprenticeship at Herd & Mackenzie in Buckie as an apprentice joiner. I started in the February of 1940 but because I was still not 15 years old I had to wait until May before beginning my apprenticeship time proper. James Herd was in charge of the yard, Tom Mackenzie was a bit older and he was on the engineering side. John H Mackenzie was an engineer in the yard, working in his overalls. He was made foreman after the first minesweeper was built.

My main job to start with was in the joiners shop and in the drafting loft in Findochty. My father was a cooper by trade, but because the fishing fleet had become part of the war effort, they did not need the herring barrels as much, so he worked in the yard manhandling the timber that was delivered. The timber was all piled up in a place we called the Meadows, a lorry would arrive and the timber would be off-loaded by man-handling it off the Lorries and piling it up outside the yard and across the road. It was back-breaking work as we used a lot of oak timbers and they were heavy.

I worked with Sam Smith who was my journeyman, our job was on the minesweepers that were being built for the Admiralty, we built the bulkheads in each of the boats. There were five main bulkheads on each boat. The knees were fitted by shipwrights but we had to dress them ready for them to fit. A knee is the shaped piece of wood about 30 inches long and 5 to 6 inches thick, it was attached by bolts to the beam timbers and right out through the hull of the boat and gave the boat extra strength.

Before we could get started to build bulkheads we had to get the Oregon Pine from across the road, where my father and his work-mates had unloaded it and take it by barrow to the Sawyer; he would cut it into planks then it would go to the circular saw for further cutting before being manually fed into the planer which finished it off. It was then ready for use.

As the years went by more and more machines were introduced which cut the back breaking work of off-loading the timbers, this was dealt with by a steam driven crane, the planer got a automatic feeder and cut out the manual pushing it took to get through the planer.

Each bulkhead was built with a 5 foot by 3 inch thick Oregon Pine plank of wood every sixteen inches along the beam of the boat, this was then strengthened by diagonals across at a 45 degree angle on each side of the bulk head, cotton was then attached to the bulkheads and this was coated in Linseed oil to make it water-tight

Two further bulkheads were constructed at the battery room and these ran fore and aft, the batteries were huge and needed to be kept as near the centre of the boat as possible.

There was obviously a very late modification called for by the Admiralty, we had to cut out holes in the bulkheads and knees to allow for a thick electrical cable to be passed round the entire circumference from stem to stern of the boat. It was obviously to do with the job of the ship in sweeping for mines and was a recent innovation.

The electrical work for this modification was completed by a Glasgow company; they ran a de-gaussing circuit all round the entire boat, a thick copper cable the thickness of your wrist was then run right round the inside hull of the boat from the engine room and back to the engine room. The batteries were connected by flat strips of copper which had again needed holes in the bulkheads as they were so big.

The batteries were being run for trials at the time we were still making holes in the bulkheads to accommodate the copper wire, it was sometimes a very difficult job as we had to fit in tiny little spaces with a hammer and chisel to enable the holes to be cut.   On one occasion I swung my hammer and a huge flash went up in the tiny space I was in, I had struck a live wire and the hammer had taken the full force of the blow. I was uninjured but the hammer still has the scars on its head to show the damage done. Health and Safety was not thought about too much, a war was on and each man had to look out for his own health and safety.

James Slater 'Gray' was married to one of my aunties, he was in the Royal Naval Reserve as a skipper during the second world war, he was sent over to Halifax, Nova Scotia to pick up Canadian built minesweepers the same type as we were building in Buckie. They had to run the checks to make sure the boat was ready for action and complete the final acceptance trials for each.   Once they had successfully completed this they secured all the loose minesweeping gear they could on the ship to enable it to make an easier passage for their trip back across the Atlantic. Having stowed most of the equipment away or secured it all on deck they went out on their last run-ashore in the town of Halifax before they were due to sail the next day. In the meantime the Canadians had received intelligence that the approaches to Halifax had been mined by the Germans and they took matters into their own hands, shifted the minesweepers to a dock area and began to put the gear back together to make it operational and thus be able to sweep for the mines laid by the Germans.

In 1944 I was called up to the army and joined the Royal Armoured Corps, most of my service was in India.

I was made up to the rank of sergeant fairly quickly and was released just after the war finished; I found out later that James Herd had signed a request seeking my return to my old job at Herd & Mackenzie. I still have all my army papers, pay book etc and my notice of early release from the Army.

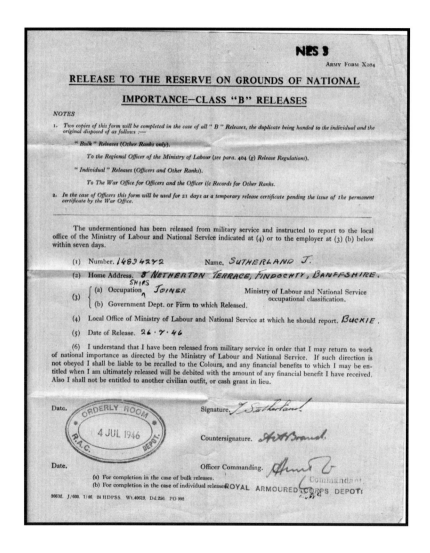

This was a form which was used for people in the armed forces who were required back at their jobs as soon as possible in order to get the country back on its feet. They had the skills to build the country back up after the war. James

Herd had applied for Joe Sutherland to return to his job as he was desperate for joiners to work in the yard.

By the time I was 22 I was back working for Herd & Mackenzie I was welcomed back into the yard, my first job was to go and see James Herd the boss so I could get my instructions. He welcomed me back and said "Jist get yer tools together ma loon and get back to work".

As I started, the fishing boat Moravia was completing her final trials, she was a Lossiemouth Boat.

I went back to work with Sam Smith and James Campbell. James Campbell had left the yard before the war and went to South Africa to stay; he had his own joiners business there. He came back to the area in 1940 to marry his girl-friend who was from Portknockie, he was not allowed to return to South Africa as he was still a British National and his skills were required for war purposes.

After the Moravia was completed there was a run of three boats with the Ashgrove, the Beechgrove and the Cedar Grove all being build for an Aberdeen company. They were built using the same format as we had for the 75 feet long wartime M.F.V's (Motorised fishing vessels).

The Melita was the first boat on which I built the cabin (crews living quarters) completely on my own. The fishermen always looked first at the cabin as it was considered to be more important than the rest of the boat. If the cabin was OK then it went a long way to the likely acceptance of the finalised boat.

In 1959 I was promoted to foreman joiner by John H Mackenzie who was now in charge of the company. I was in charge of the joinery department along with Sam Smith. I trained all the apprentices to be good tradesmen. I had my own high standards and I tried to instill the pride I felt in my work on the apprentices

I was responsible for training. They were all good lads and I was very proud of each of them as they turned out to be the best tradesmen around.

That was brought home to me by a recent meeting (Summer 2006) with John Buchan who was the yard foreman of Jones Shipyard, our rivals but friendly rivals it must be said as we all got on. I was out for a walk with my neighbour when John pulled up in his car for a chat, he said to me at one point

"Joe, you built up the finest group of tradesmen that has ever been, I don't think the like will ever be seen again"

It was an extremely nice thing to say and I was very proud that someone like John Buchan recognised that they were all good tradesmen.

In July 1970 my friend and mentor of many years retired from Herd & Mackenzie, Sam Smith had given many years of his life to the company and we men in the joiners shop presented him with a farewell present.

L to R Jim Murray – John W Smith – Edwin Flett – Fred Murray – Alan Fowler – Leslie Work – John Clark – Hamish Carter –Charlie McGillivary – John Bruce– Alex T. Sutherland – Joe Sutherland. In front are Sam Smith being presented his gift by **Michael Fettes the youngest apprentice.**

The Bonaventure and the Rebecca were two boats which I think of with great pride, they were at the pinnacle of quality workmanship. I was extremely pleased with both boats which were destined for Eyemouth. The craftsmanship was wonderful and the joiners excelled themselves with these boats, they were a credit to the yard.

Herd & Mackenzie was a very happy place to work and our clients said that to me on a number of occasions that it was such a friendly place to be in. I would endorse that and I felt privileged to work there with a bunch of fine men and women.

CAPTAIN SCOTT

The very mention of the name conjures up an image of a courageous Antarctic explorer who died in his efforts to become the first man to reach the South Pole. However, in the seafaring town of Buckie any mention of the Captain Scott turn thoughts immediately to the 'other' Captain Scott.

This particular Captain Scott did indeed get its name from the famous explorer but was 'born' many years after his death in 1912; she came alive in the highly skilled boat building yard of Herd & Mackenzie based in Buckie. The ship was to bear the proud name and was to stand for all the good qualities held by Captain Scott of the Antarctic.

Some 50 years after Scott's adventure in the South Pole the Dulverton Trust began to look at providing adventure training for young men between the ages of sixteen and twenty one. They finally came up with three criteria that they believed would assist young men of that age to reach adulthood having tested themselves in differing situations

---

1. The main object should be to give the maximum opportunity for a young man to discover his real potential and to establish confidence in himself.

2. The best way of achieving this object should be through a combination of experience at sea and expeditions in the mountains of Scotland and Wales.

3. To gain the maximum effect, courses must extend to 26 days in duration as anything less is likely to achieve disproportionately disappointing results.

The answer to their own objectives was to have the Schooner Captain Scott built to carry out the specific role of an Adventure Training Sailing Ship and from then on much thought went into her design and into the yard that woud construct her.

The race to build such a craft was very competitive; to have the facility, the skilled workers and the vision to build such a ship that would grace the seas and be a lasting memorial to the men who conceived and built her, was a prize that any shipyard would love to have.

Herd & Mackenzie won the contract, it was a very proud moment for John Mackenzie and his work force. Together they would create this ship and they would build a ship the likes of which had never been constructed in many a long year. The founders of the shipyard had witnessed at close quarters the completion of the Cutty Sark in their early days at Denny's shipyard in Dumbarton, no doubt that vision would have been carried north with them to Findochty. They worked hand in hand with their skilled craftsmen at Buckie to build beautifully crafted wooden boats for the rigours of fishing in the north seas. Those early craftsmen in turn passed their skills to the generations that followed, until in 1971 they were given the ultimate challenge to build this ship.

The result was a magnificient sea boat, able to sail in all weathers at all times of the year both in open sea and in close waters.

This wooden ship was a beautifully crafted jewel, hand built by a team of men who had a long history of building boats from wood. She was built by men who were proud of the skills they had, who were delighted to be given the chance of showing the world that they could still build beautiful sailing craft which would equal the likes of the Cutty Sark.

When the idea of this book was first mooted it was obvious that those given the task would have the advantage of talking face to face with the man who stood so long as the guiding light of Herd & Mackenzie having taken over from his father and uncle before their deaths in 1951. The valuable time he was able to give to the project added much to the story of the shipyard. That apart it was a genuine pleasure for those who had never met him to speak to the man who radiated enthusiasm even in his advanced years.

John Mackenzie, the owner of the yard until his retiral in 1979, had in his possession an order book dating back to 1903 in which every ship, boat, yacht and minesweeper is diligently recorded. So it was with the Captain Scott

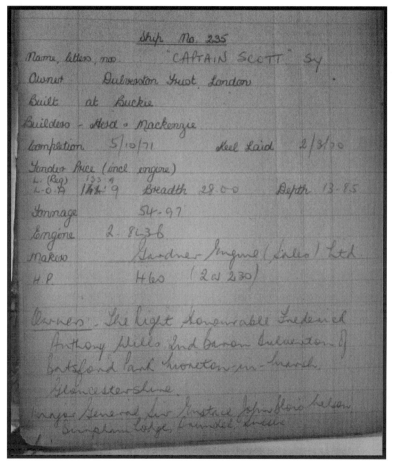

The above photograph of the original order book gives all the shorthand version of the detail for the ship on one single page.

Herd & Mackenzie had won the prize and gained the contract, it was a staggering success for the men of the ship yard, they could visualise the finished article and were exceptionally keen to get started. They would be putting all their skills to good use in creating a ship that would be the pride of the yard, the pride of the Moray coast and indeed the pride of Scotland.

In an interview with John H Mackenzie he said;-

The first contact I had regarding the building of the Captain Scott was when two representatives of a trust came to see if our yard was suitable for building a wooden sailing ship of approximately 150 feet in length, and if so, would we be interested in building such a ship.

I said that we would most definitely be as we had all the facilities and the best wooden boat builders in the country to carry out such work, but unfortunately, we knew nothing about sails. They said this would be no problem as they could arrange this. When I asked they told me they represented a trust, but could not name it at that time and went on to say that they had representatives going around various yards both in this country and on the continent to find the most suitable yard.

I invited them to go round the yard and see the type of work we were doing and to make their minds up as to whether or not we were capable of undertaking what they had in mind. They came back from their tour full of enthusiasm and told me the trustees would be meeting in two days time and they would let me know the result.

They called me after the meeting to say they had decided we would be the builders and asked when we could start work. They then told me the owners were to be the Dulverton Trust. I was most surprised to be told we were to be the preferred builders as I had never seen any specification, the only thing being a small outline of a three- masted sailing ship and I had only given them an 'out of the hat' ideas as to possible cost. I was given an assurance that all was in order and for me to proceed with the work and confirmation would be sent straight away with a confirmatory cheque.

We proceeded to build a ship that we were all justifiably proud of, being a thing of beauty and the biggest wooden sailing ship in the world, as far as I know. She was built as a character-training vessel under the command of Commander Victor Clark DSC* R.N. Rtd. who proved to be the ideal man for the job.

After years of good service in this country, she was sold to the Sultan of Oman and is used for training young men for the Omani Navy. She has sailed the oceans of the world and has visited all the Baltic countries, Australia and America and is still doing good work.

The specially selected wood used to build this fine ship had, first, to be weathered; nothing like a Scottish winter to ensure it gets a proper wintering.

The snow covered timbers lie in the Herd & Mackenzie Yard at Buckie – weathering in the winter months – it is difficult to imagine how this pile of wood could possibly be turned into such a beautiful ship as the Captain Scott.

The yard managers spent some months planning the project which meant identifying material sources, ordering the right type of timber for the various jobs ahead. Using all their skills to muster together the ingredients required for such a fine ship. Right from the start they would need the vision to 'see' in their minds eye the finished article. A ship that would grace any sea, a ship that would be seaworthy in all weathers, a ship they could all be very proud of, a unique and sleek wooden ship that would turn the eye of any mariner.

The oak beams had to be weathered in readiness for their various tasks onboard. None was more important than those of the keel that was fashioned from six of these massive pieces of oak.

The keel was be laid on 2nd March 1970 and denoted a particular land-mark in the ship's life.

With the wood selected, seasoned and weathered, it was time for the shipwrights to get to work and get the timbers ready for the important role in the ships life as the keel.

The keel is laid with Magnus Work, Alan Towns and George Cowie
utilising their skills to align the keel.

The Captain elect, Commander Victor Clark inspects the keel as it is laid ready for the ship to be built. Looking on is John H Mackenzie in the hat and Alex. Smith in the 'bunnet'

The interest shown in the building of the Captain Scott by its owners the Dulverton Trust was evident. Constant visits to the yard were made by various interested parties, not in any way to ensure that all was well, but to watch the ship rise from the stocks and turn from the ugly lumps of wood into a thing of beauty. Quite what was going through the mind of Victor Clark when he visited and viewed the keel is not obvious to the layman. No doubt his sailor's mind would have been working overtime.

Time was always made for any visitor from the Dulverton trust to come to the yard and see how their ship was progressing. People of all walks of life who had connections with the company and who had previously little or no knowledge of how such a boat was put together, would turn up at the yard. They would be taken on a tour of the yard and all the mysteries of the construction would be explained to them in words they could understand with their limited knowledge of ship building.

Alan Towns and Alexander Farquhar set to work preparing the keel timbers

The base of every ship built is the keel, that backbone of the ship is the centrepiece. All the other timbers take their lead from the keel and every care has to be taken that it will withstand all the strains and stresses that will be laid upon it for the remainder of the ship's life. Huge pieces of oak are shaped in such a way as to strengthen each other as they are laid in the line that will hold up the rest of the ship and give her the strength to withstand all weathers.

Yard Joint General Manager John Clark

What is happening here is that John Clark is checking the 'through fastenings' These are the pilot bolts ¾ inches in diameter and 18" long which are driven through from the outside hull and riveted to the internal hull timbers. Remember he is the yard joint general manager and yet here he is just checking to make sure the bolts and rivets are in place and secure on the Captain Scott.

George Cowie busy caulking the deck timbers of the Captain Scott

Fred Murray and his apprentice George Cormack get the decking laid in the crews quarters

General description of the Captain Scott

The ship is a three masted topgallant yard schooner, 144 ft and 3 inches in length, 28 ft beam and displacing 380 tons. She has a draft of 15 ft, the length to the jib boom end is 171 feet with the length on the waterline coming in at 129 feet.

The planking is 3 ¼ inch thick Scottish Larch below the waterline and 2 ¾ inch thick above, she has 4 inch thick planks on the sheer and bilge strakes. The frames are 5 inch thick sided Oak.

Robert Clark of Hull designed the hull which has the appearance of a traditional Trading Schooner above water but the shape underwater owes more to yacht design.

The masts and rigging were designed by Michael Willoughby, who was a one time master of the Sir Winston Churchill. He knew just what was required to rig the ship in such a way that she would sail along in the wind with as much sail as she could muster and at a rate of knots that would gladden the heart.

The masts were manufactured by Sparlight Ltd of Hampshire and the Captain Scott was rigged by Harry Spencer of Cowes. These masts, with the main truck 98 ft and 5 inches above the deck, carry ten fore and aft sails and four square sails on the foremast. The lower masts are constructed in aluminium and the topmasts and other spars are in spruce, they were made by Clark & Carter.

When fully rigged with all sails the master will have 9097 square feet of canvas, the sails were made by Ratsey & Lapthron.

The ship is fitted with two 230 horse power Gardner diesel auxiliary engines driving twin screw which have the capability of being 'feathered' by hand to reduce resistance when sailing.

Part of the work force from Herd & Mackenzie who helped in her construction

In the water without her masts and rigging – A lady only half dressed! She is ready to have her masts and sailing rig put in place – her lines already showing the lines of the beautiful ship she has become.

Under the banner headline of "The splendour of a bygone maritime age recaptured at Buckie" the local paper The Banffshire Advertiser proudly waxed lyrical about the achievement of the ship that Herd & Mackenzie had created in their yard at Buckie.

A magnificent example of Buckie skill and craftsmanship - the three masted adventure training schooner Captain Scott was launched in brilliant sunshine at Buckie on Tuesday (7th September 1971) from the yard of her builders Messrs Herd & Mackenzie. It was a splendid and very impressive occasion with the tall proud ship, completely dominating the scene with her grace and beauty and recapturing all the splendour of a bygone maritime age, slid smoothly into the water in a highly efficient operation that took less than ten minutes to complete.

Installing the main mast with Herbert Wright and Willie Milne
of Herd & Mackenzie assisting the riggers from Harry Spencer as the
mainmast is lowered into position through the deck.

"I name this ship Captain Scott, may God bless her and all who sail in her"
From left Victor Clark, John Mackenzie, Lady Nelson, Mary Mackenzie, Peter Scott and Sir John Nelson
(chairman of the schooner committee of the Locheil Trust)

A crowd estimated at between 2000 - 3000 people turned out to watch the spectacle, standing rows deep round the harbour and facing on to the shipyard and occupying the many other vantage points on the high ground overlooking the harbour. The ceremony began with the blessing of the ship and a prayer for all who would sail on her - delivered in a simple but very appropriate service conducted by the very Reverend Hugh Douglas a former moderator of the Church of Scotland, and Reverend Gordon Clark, whose brother, Commander Victor Clark R.N., is to be master of the vessel. Then came the official naming performed by Lady Jane Nelson wife of Major-General Sir John Nelson, chairman of the schooner committee of the Loch Eil Trust, who are to operate the Captain Scott and, as the ship at once began to glide down the launching rails on her cradle, two pipers standing at the waters edge, Pipe Major Albert Sim and Lance Corporal Arnie Flett both from Kirkwall, Orkney - played the tune "Morar Sym" the march past of the Lovat Scouts, followed by the "Skye Boat Song". Commissioned by the Dulverton Trust, the 380 ton schooner, named after the famous Antarctic explorer, Captain Robert Falcon Scott, will be the largest British sailing ship at sea with 14 sails giving her 9000 square feet of canvas in full rig. She took 18 months to build and fit out and, after completing her trials in the Moray Firth off Buckie during the next three weeks, she will sail for her base at Plockton, Wester Ross. From there she will operate 26 day adventure and sail training cruises combined with expeditions ashore for youths aged 16 - 21. The cruises will take in the Western Isles, Orkney, Shetland, the Irish coast and St Kilda far out in the Atlantic. Thirty six young men will be accommodated on each course at a fee of £90 per head and nine courses a year are planned, the first of these on October 18th 1971. Following Tuesday's launching about 170 guests attended a luncheon given by the builders and the Dulverton Trust in Cullen Town Hall during which Lady Nelson was presented with an inscribed goblet in Caithness glass with a replica of Captain Scott carved on it. The gift, in recognition of her services, was handed over by Mrs Mary Mackenzie, wife of Mr John H. Mackenzie, managing director of the shipyard who presided.

Pipe Major Albert Sim and Lance Corporal Arnie Flett both from Kirkwall, Orkney – played the tune "Morar Sym" the march past of the Lovat Scouts, followed by the "Skye Boat Song".

Commander Peter Scott RN Retd. Leads the crowds in giving three cheers

Lt Cdr Victor Clark & Cdr Peter Scott discuss the finer points of the Captain Scott

The windlass set up for'ard

In proposing a toast to the ship and her owners, the Dulverton Trust, Mr Mackenzie said that his firm had built many different types of vessels in their seventy years in business but the Captain Scott was by far the most interesting of all. Referring to the choice of name for the schooner, Mr Mackenzie said that 'Scott of the Antarctic' was a man who, in the face of hardship and danger, had proved himself to be a born leader of men and an inspiration to all young people. "After his untimely death" he went on "a wooden cross was erected overlooking the great ice barrier as a memorial to Captain Scott and his companions who died with him, on which was carved the following words "to strive; to seek; to find and not yield" declared Mr Mackenzie; "Could any adventure training vessel have a better motto or a better name"?

John H Mackenzie C.B.E. meets Peter Markham Scott, C.H, C.B.E, D.S.C, F.R.S F. Z. S.

Mr Mackenzie said they were delighted to have present with them on this occasion the famous explorers son, naturalist Commander Peter Scott R.N.   Mr Mackenzie made special reference to the Trustees of the Dulverton Trust who had made the venture possible, "since the meeting of Lord Dulverton and members of the Schooner Committee under the chairmanship of Sir John Nelson" he said "I have formed the highest regard for them, they are doing a great work encouraging young people and providing the facilities to help them become worthy citizens in this troubled world"

In the water at last but not yet free – on launch day September 1971

Replying to the toast, Lord Dulverton paid tribute to the skill and craftsmanship of the men who had built the Captain Scott, and said that he and the trustees believed that the ship had a very important contribution to make in the training of young people, he also referred to the very generous backing they were to receive from the MacRobert trust in running the venture, toasting the builders, Commander Peter Scott said it had been an extremely moving and impressive occasion and described the whole ceremony as "a masterpiece of organisation."

Like Lord Dulverton he also believed that the Captain Scott had a tremendous role to play and he hoped that the expeditions planned for those who sailed on her would include natural history as one of the elements. Mr Jack Herd, director of the firm, replied on behalf of the builders.

There were nine cruises per year; they all started on a Monday with 36 trainees joining the ship. 36 people from all walks of life, about a dozen of them privately paid for; the others were from a wide spectrum of businesses, the police, army cadet forces, education authorities or individual schools.

The first two days were spent on the ship at her mooring buoy, this allowed the trainees to get familiar with the ship, learn basic seamanship, going through the emergency drills for lifeboat and fire. The learned about boat handling, the rigging, the Ship's wheel, anchors and cables. Fitness was emphasised every single day with a climb to the crosstrees after breakfast each morning and other exercises throughout the day.

The Navigation table on the bridge

After that gentle introduction it was time to get underway, and the third day saw the schooner use her powerful engines to sail from their base at the Loch Eil Trust at Achdaliel on the short journey to Fort William where the months' provisions were embarked. Once that all important task was complete, it was time to see what kind of sailors the trainees would make. The ship made for the relatively calm inland waters around the Island of Mull for the first sailing practice.

The sails were hoisted by muscle power alone, an extremely difficult and strength sapping job. The trainees would have to get used to the hard work needed to get the sails up the huge masts as they were the 'engines' used on most occasions. They had to learn about tacking, gybing, trimming the yards, hauling taut the sheets and reefing, all this had to be learned before the mate could be satisfied the crew could safely handle the sails in open seas around the Outer Hebrides.

The Galley in action

The volunteer yardsmen, hanging on at the top yard over a heaving sea needed clear heads and strong hands. No cruise passed without encountering a full gale at some stage, in the winter cruises these gales were a much more frequent occurrence with one gale succeeding another for four weeks.

The dizzying heights that the volunteer crew had to contend with in open sea in all weathers

The boys soon overcame their sea sickness but they found that life at sea has other discomforts. Extreme fatigue, all you want to do is to lie down in your bunk as you are at the end of your energy, but the mate wants you aloft to handle heavy wet sails, you are soaking wet, your hands are blistered and the salt spray is stinging your face as you climb the yardarm. This is what the sailors in days gone by had to put up with when sailing the seas on schooners just like the Captain Scott. The ships were made of oak and the men were made of steel. Toughened by the conditions under which they had to perform. This is what made the best seamen in the world in days of yore and it was hoped that this experience would help these young men of today become better able to handle the conditions they would have to encounter in a modern world.

It was not all gales and blisters however; a gentle cruise followed round the Outer Hebrides with just a fresh breeze helping the Captain Scott glide through the short waves. With nothing but the creak of the rigging and the bright splash of the bow wave under the bowsprit that housed the carved figure of Captain Robert Scott, fully kitted out in his Antarctic gear. Sometimes the ship would anchor in a loch for the night; the crew were still required to man the various positions on the ship at anchor.

In addition to the sea time, the crew had three shore expeditions during their cruise, the logistics of getting all of the crew ashore with provisions and equipment to get them through two and a half days over rough country was not an easy task. The crew would be under the supervision of their instructors for the first two days which had them trekking across hills, down glens and through forests before camping overnight in the heather. The third and last expedition ashore would have the crew being given a planned route to complete without the close support of their instructors.

The course would end on a Saturday; four weeks after she had set off from Achdalieu with the Captain of the ship took her back to her mooring buoy under sail with no aid from the engines. It was a triumphal return and a tribute to the crew that they could handle the ship under sail power to allow the Captain to sail right up to the buoy.

The Captain Scott in all her glory.

Captain Scott – The Explorer

No article about Captain Scott would be complete without recourse to the great man himself. He perished along with his gallant fellows in the cause of exploration. His instantly recognisable name was given to the one of the most beautiful ships ever launched.

The very name sends out a powerful message, Captain Robert Falcon Scott was born on the 6th June 1868 in the village of Stoke Damerel near Devonport Devon. He left home at thirteen years of age and joined the Royal Navy as a midshipman; he served on several Royal Navy warships rising rapidly through the ranks.

He was given command of the HMS Discovery the ship that would take the National Antarctic Expedition 1901 – 1904 on a voyage of exploration of the Ross Sea.

The land to the east of the ice sea was sighted for the first time and named "**King Edward VII Land**" in honour of the then monarch the Polar Plateau was discovered and a new "furthest south" was achieved by Scott.

Captain Robert Falcon Scott 1868 - 1912

It was evident that he enjoyed being in command of the Antarctic expedition. He returned home after his exploration of the Polar Plateau in 1902 and started immediately to raise the necessary finance to return to the Antarctic and to realise his ambition to be the first to get to the South Pole. On the 14th September 1908 he married Edith Agnes Kathleen Bruce. His first and only son Peter Markham Scott was born exactly a year after his parents wedding on 14th September 1909. He was to achieve fame as a distinguished ornothologist and painter.

It took nearly eight years for Scott to be able to mount his second expedition to the Antarctic on the Terra Nova.

Terra Nova

They sailed for the Antarctic and heard enroute that Amundsen was also heading in the same direction with the same goal in mind. It was a 'race for the pole'.

The Terra Nova was not as strong a ship as his rival's which was specially built to withstand the ice further south. This meant that Amundsen could take his ship 100 km nearer to the location of the pole with his rival Scott having to traverse that distance with his party of five men.

The full party was Captain Scott, Lieutenant Henry Bowers, Doctor Henry Wilson, Army captain Lawrence Oates and Petty officer Edgar Evans had made the gallant effort and reached the South pole on January 17th/18th of 1912.

What they found was that Amundsen had reached the pole a month earlier.

Amunsden and his party had returned to their base alive and well whereas the five men in Scott's part perished on their return journey to their base. It had been a huge and heroic effort by Scott and his men but it had cost them their lives.

The First Captain of the Captain Scott

Lt. Commander Victor Clark D.S.C * R.N. Retd.

Victor Cecil Froggat Clark was born at Dover on 24th May 1908, he was a son of the manse, his father being The vicar of Bromley-by-Bow. He was educated at Haileybury near Hertford. He spent his school holidays on Lowestoft fishing sail boats and it is this early baptism at sea that gave him his love for the sea and sail boats.

He enlisted in the Royal Navy as a midshipman and during the 1930s saw service onboard the battleships HMS Valiant and HMS Warspite and the destroyer HMS Anthony.

His other passion was motor bikes, of which he owned a few despite knowing little about the workings of engines. He explored far and wide including the Holy Land.

In 1938 he was at Greenock where his next ship was being built, he was the First Lieutenant aboard the HMS Punjabi a Tribal class destroyer and was involved in the Battle of Narvik on 13th April 1940 when HMS Warspite and her consorts destroyed eight enemy warships and a U Boat. The Punjabi had suffered heavy casualties and damage but was back with the fleet in time to take part in the evacuation of troops from the raid on St Nazaire. Following St Nazaire he was awarded the Distinguished Service Cross (D.S.C.)

His war service continued with a brief spell in command of his old ship HMS Anthony, this ended when the ship was damaged in rough weather.

Clark was posted to HMS Repulse which was sunk when she and the battleship Prince of Wales were attacked by Japanese war planes.

H.M.S. REPULSE

The two battleships formed the core of Force Z and both were sunk in the South China Sea on 10th December 1941 when they were attacked by 27 bombers and 61 Torpedo planes. The Repulse was hit by five torpedoes and sank quickly with the loss of 513 men.

Clark had been at his action station on A Turret, these 15 inch guns were not used in the attack by the Japanese aircraft, when the ship started going down and Abandon Ship was broadcast, Clark managed to get off and swim to a life-raft.

He was picked up by escorting destroyers and returned to Singapore where he was posted to Combined Headquarters in Singapore. He joined forces with Major Angus Rose of the Argyll & Sutherland Highlanders and between them they took command of a flotilla of gunboats manned by around 50 Royal Marines and 50 Australian Army volunteers.

The motley force began operations against the advancing Japanese army who had swept down the Malaysian peninsula and were nearing Singapore. The Allied forces were under constant attack and retreated to the south to Batu Pahat. His force volunteered to take the river gunboats Dragonfly and Scorpion to attempt a rescue of 2000 Australian, Indian and British troops who were cut off and almost encircled by Japanese troops.

The operation lasted four nights but the soldiers were brought out and taken to waiting ships and the then comparative safety of Singapore.

Clark was sent to Java with a motor launch and 60 troops to continue his guerrilla raids on the Japanese forces, however as he entered the Durian Strait he found his way blocked by a Japanese destroyer.

His launch was armed with a four pound gun and small arms but undeterred he launched his boat at the destroyer closing to within 400 yards and opened fire with every weapon on board.

The enemy returned fire and blasted the launch to virtual loss with fires taking hold in the engine room and his four pounder gun knocked out of action, the rudder had gone and the launch was sinking fast.

Clark swam ashore and eventually landed at Sumatra, he joined with others of his crew and they spent a couple of months in deep jungle before being betrayed by the locals and taken prisoner by the Japanese.

He spent the next three and half years in a prisoner of war camp at Palembang under the Japanese. During that time he received a Red Cross parcel from his mother who told him that he had been award a Bar to his D.S.C. His courage and daring were without question.

In 1945 he was transferred to Changi jail on Singapore where he was liberated from when Japanese forces were defeated.

Clark went home and was given command of the frigate Loch Tralaig; that ended when he ran her aground off the Isle of Arran.

He then spent five years as chief training officer to the Sea Cadets during which he planned his next adventure of a circumnavigation. He bought a nine-ton ketch called *Solace* and his 40.000 miles voyage began following his retiral from the Royal Navy in 1953.

The next six years he spent on the *Solace* with only a West Indian boy, Stanley Mathurin, as the only other crew. They spent nine months shipwrecked on the atoll of Palmerston in the Cook Islands but with the help of the descendants of a master cooper who had colonised the atoll in the 19th Century, he was able to repair the *Solace* and continue his voyage.

In 1962 he took command of the Outward Bound schooner Prince Louis and it was then he came up with the idea of having a sail training ship for young people. With his friend Dr Kurt Hahn they began to lobby in an attempt to get the idea off the stocks. They enlisted the assistance of the Duke of Edinburgh and soon the Dulverton Trust was making studies into the viability of the idea.

Clark and Hahn joined with Lord Dulverton and they began to plan the project which led to the building of the Captain Scott at the yard of Herd & Mackenzie in Buckie.

Lieutenant Commander Clark was given the command of the newly built schooner and he took command for three years in 1971 until 1974.

He married Danae Stileman in 1975 when he was aged 67 and she 34 years of age. After his time on the Captain Scott he went on to teach at the Emsworth Sailing School.

He was the author of two books one was an account of his voyage on the Solace and was titled "On the wings of a dream" published in 1960 and the second his life story entitled "Triumph and Disaster" in 1994.

Lieutenant Commander Victor Clark D.S.C. * (R.N. Retd.) died aged 97 on the 14th December 2005 he is survived by his wife and daughters.

John Mackenzie only learned of the death of his old friend during his interviews for this book in late 2006 and was visibly upset. He had formed a good friendship with Victor Clark during their time working together on the Captain Scott.

Victor Clark at the launch of the Captain Scott in 1971

The boats built by Herd & Mackenzie

No record of the achievements of the workforce at Herd & Mackenzie would be complete without a detailed reference to the boats they built.

One of the co-authors of this book, John Addison, has compiled a complete historical record of every single boat built by Herd & Mackenzie from Findochty to Buckie and at Peterhead.

He has photographs for many of them and they are included. He shares this with us all. It is a fitting tribute to all of the men who worked for the yard; from its beginnings in 1903 when three young men had a dream.

The boats speak for themselves; sturdy craft crewed by strong and dependable men who had one of the toughest jobs in the world. They complemented each other and relied on each other, the boats were good sea boats and the seamen on the boats were good sailors who knew their craft.

It is impossible to try and calculate the sea mileage that all of the boats covered during their active lives. They were involved in many other roles other than fishing and I am sure many of the fishermen had more than once thanked the men of Herd & Mackenzie who had built their boats which brought them safely home.

VALLAR CROWN   BF 249
Yard No 2   year 1906   owner J.W.Cowie Portessie
Loa.ft / m 82.4ft / 25.1 m   Brth ft / m 18 ft / 5.4 m   Dpth ft / m 8.5ft / 2.5 m
Engine Hp / kw 16 inch compound 26hp
History 1922--------1950 various owners 1950 scrapped

EXCELSIOR   BF 683
Yard No 5   year   1907   owner J.Duguid & A.Slater Portessie
Loa.ft / m 86.1ft / 26.24 m   Brth ft / m 18.1ft / 5.51 m Dpth ft / m 8.7ft / 2.65 m
Engine Hp / kw   16inch compound, 30hp / 22kw
History 1915-1920 war service, 1929 BCK 35, 1933 scrapped

BONCHIEF   BCK 17
Yard No 9   year 1908   owner   A & G Herd Findochty
Loa.ft / m 86.6ft/26.6 m   Brth ft / m 18.3ft / 5.5 m   Dpth ft / m 9.1ft / 2.77m
engine Hp / kw   16inch compound 28hp
History1916-----1919 war service, 1949 scrapped

DOCILE III   BCK 70
Yard No 13   year   1910   owner   W.Flett & J.Flett Findochty
Loa.ft / m 86.2ft / 26.2 m   Brth ft / m 18.9ft / 5.6 m   Dpth ft / m   9.4ft / 2.86 m
engine Hp / kw   16 inch compound 27hp
History 1916---1920 war service, 1919 owner W Findlay Cullen, 1936 scrapped

HOME FRIEND   BCK 89
Yard No 14   year 1911   owner J.& W. Legge, & J.Flett Findochty
Loa.ft / m 87.8ft / 26.7 m   Brth ft / m 18.6 ft / 5.6 m   Dpth ft / m 9.1 ft / 2.7 m
Engine Hp / kw 16 inch compound 24hp
History 1915---1920 war service, 1931 owner A.McKay Sandend BF 257, 1939 scrapped

OBTAIN   BCK 355
Yard No 32   year 1917   owner W.Findlay Cullen
Loa.ft / m90.8ft / 27.6 m   Brth ft / m 19.4ft / 5.9 m   Dpth ft / m 9.5ft / 2.89 m
Engine Hp / kw 18inch triple expansion, 27hp / 20kw
History 1917---1919, 1940----1945 war service, 1945 Rose Valley BF 80, 1948 PD 22,
1952 scrapped

H M D SOLSTICE

Yard No 33   year 1918   owner Admiralty
Loa.ft / m 87 ft/ 26.5 m   Brth ft / m 20 ft / 6.09 m   Dpth ft / m 10.2 ft / 3.1 m
Engine Hp / kw 18 inch triple expansion 43 hp
History 1920 INS 276, 1930 BF 140, 1939–1946 war service,1948 scrapped

H M D SUNSPOT

Yard No 35   year 1920   owner Admiralty
Loa.ft / m 87.6 ft / 26.7 m Brth ft / m 19.8 ft / 6.03 m   Dpth ft / m 10.3 ft / 3.19 m
Engine Hp   18 inch triple expansion   33 hp
History 1921 INS317, 1938 Mary Johnston BF 15, 1940–1946 war service, 1951 scrapped

LIZZIE WEST   BF 213
Yard No 39   year 1930   owner J.West Gardenstown
Loa.ft / m 90.6 ft / 27.6 m   Brth ft / m 20 ft / 6.09m   Dpth ft / m 10.1 ft / 3.07m
Engine Hp   18 inch triple expansion   34hp
History 1941-1945 war service,1944 M 2, 1946 LT 495,1961 Barking vessel at Fraserburgh,
1968 scrapped .

JOHN HERD   FR 149
Yard No 40   year 1930   owner John Herd Fraserburgh
Loa.ft / m91.9 ft / 28.01m Brth ft / m 20.1 ft / 6.12 m   Dpth ft / m 9.9 ft / 3.01m
Engine Hp 18 inch triple expansion 43hp
History 1940---1945 war service, 1946 BF 94, 1951 scrapped

NAUTILUS   BCK 7
Yard No 38   year 1929   owner G.A.Smith Portessie
Loa.ft / m65ft / 19.8 m   Brth ft / m 18.5 ft / 5.6m Dpth ft / m8.6 ft / 2.6 m
Engine Hp / kw 95hp / 70.8 kw Gardner
History 30/11/41 lost on war service at Dunkirk

LIBERTY   BF 429
Yard No 42   year 1932   owner J.Addison Cullen
Loa.ft / m 56ft / 17.06m Brth ft / m 15ft / 4.57m   Dpth ft / m 5ft / 1.5 m

CELERITY   BCK 142
Yard No 43   year   1933   owner   A.Bruce Findochty
Loa.ft / m 56ft / 17.06m   Brth ft / m 16ft / 4.87m   Dpth ft / m 6ft / 1.82m
Engine Hp Gardner 54hp
History 1950 LK 187,1970---1980's various owners, 1987 converted to yacht based Amsterdam

MMS 53
Yard No 77   year 1941   owner Admiralty
Loa.ft / m 105ft / 32m   Brth ft / m 22ft / 6.7m   Dpth ft / m 6ft / 1.82m
Engine Hp / kw 500hp / 372 kw Crossley
History 1945 -51 Greek Navy **Korytsa** 1-10-56 sold

MMS 1016
Yard No 83   year 1941   owner   Admiralty
Loa.ft / m 105ft / 32m   Brth ft / m   22ft / 6.7m Dpth ft / m 8ft / 2.43m
Engine Hp / kw   500hp / 372kw Harland & Wolf
History 1944 Vernon, 1945 Danish Navy, 29-1-46 wrecked Jutland

MMS   1047
Yard No 84   year 1941   owner Admiralty
Loa.ft / m 105ft / 32m   Brth ft / m   22ft / 6.7m   Dpth ft / m 8ft / 2.43m
Engine Hp / kw   500hp / 372 kw Harland & Wolf
History 22-11-46 sold

MFV 1043

Yard No 85   year 1944   owner Admiralty
Loa.ft / m 75ft / 22.8m   Brth ft / m 19.7ft / 6.01m   Dpth ft / m 9.5ft / 2.8 m
Engine Hp Blackstone 160 hp   History 1947 Kathleen Pirie A 297, 1952 Fair Morn BF
340,1957 Replenish FR   239,1976 Fair Morn FR 239, 1980 no record in Olsens Almanac

MFV 1087

Yard No 88   year   1944   owner Admiralty
Loa.ft / m 75 ft / 22.8 m   Brth ft / m 19.7 ft / 6.01   Dpth ft / m 9.5 ft / 2.8 m
Engine Hp / kw   Blackstone 160 hp / 121 kw
History 1947 Glenugie PD 340, 1956 sold to South Africa

MFV 1154
Yard No 96   year 1946   owner Admiralty
Loa.ft / m 75ft / 22.8m   Brth ft / m 19.7ft / 6.01m Dpth ft / m 9.5ft / 2.8m
Engine Hp Blackstone 160 hp
History 1946 Harvest Gleaner BCK 120, 1986 sold out of fishing

MFV 1209
Yard No 97   year 1946   owner Admiralty
Loa.ft / m 75 ft / 22.8 m   Brth ft / m 19.7 ft / 6.01 m   Dpth ft / m 9.5 ft / 2.8 m
Engine Hp / kw Blackstone 160 hp / 121 kw
History 1946 Ashgrove A 244, 1957 PD 270, 1958 Spes Clara PD 270, 1963 cargo vessel based Shetland

WINDERMERE   PD 203

Yard No 100   year   1947   owner   A..Reid Peterhead
Loa.ft / m 62.6ft / 19.08   Brth ft / m 17.6ft / 5.3m Dpth ft / m 9.3ft / 2.8m
Engine Hp / kw 114hp /85kw Gardner
History 1955 sold as a pilot boat

ARNHEM   INS 117

Yard No 101   year   1947   owner A. Campbell Lossiemouth
Loa.ft / m 62.6ft / 19.08m   Brth ft / m 18.3ft / 5.5 m   Dpth ft / m 9.3ft / 2.8 m
Engine Hp / kw   114hp / 85 kw Gardner
History 1960 Chary BF 228, 1967 BCK 243 , 1995 converted to Pleasure Boat

ORION   INS 125
Yard No 102   year 1947   owner   J.Main Nairn
Loa.ft / m 68ft / 20.7 m   Brth ft / m 17.3ft / 5.3 m Dpth ft / m 7.8ft / 2.4 m
Engine Hp / kw
History 1977 B 184, 1982 N 384, 1993 Scrapped burned on the beach Portavogie

MELITA   INS 163
Yard No 106   year 1947   owner   W.Main Burghead
Loa.ft / m 65ft / 19.81m   Brth ft / m 18ft / 5.4m   Dpth ft / m 7.8ft / 2.4m
Engine Hp / kw 120hp / 89kw Blackstone
History 1960 N 160, 2002 scrapped

AUREOLA   BCK 181
Yard No 108   year   1948   owner A. Farquhar Portessie
Loa.ft / m 65ft/19.8m   Brth ft / m   18ft / 5.4m   Dpth ft / m 9.6ft / 2.9m
Engine Hp / kw 120hp/89kw Blackstone
History 1970 B 79, 1973 Fruitful B 79, 1981 no record in Olsens Almanac

SOUVENIR   BCK 183
Yard No 109   year 1948   owner J.Clark Portessie
Loa.ft / m 67ft/ 20.4m Brth ft / m 18ft / 5.4m   Dpth ft / m 9.6ft / 2.9m
Engine Hp / kw   160hp / 119kw Blackstone
History 1963 Comet BCK 183, late 1960's sank off Wick after collision

MORAYSHIRE   INS 212
Yard No 112   year 1948   owner D.Farquhar Lossiemouth
Loa.ft / m 62ft / 18.8m   Brth ft / m 18ft / 5.4m   Dpth ft / m 9.3ft / 2.8m
Engine Hp / kw   114hp / 85kw Gardner
History 1984 sold for pleasure craft based Thames

DEVOTION   INS 223
Yard No 116   year 1949   owner J.Ralph Hopeman
Loa.ft / m 65ft / 19.8m   Brth ft / m 18ft / 5.4m   Dpth ft / m 7.4ft / 2.3m
Engine Hp / kw   114hp / 85kw Gardner
History 26th Aug 1960 wrecked Gardenstown Bay

COPIOUS   BF 211
Yard No 120   year 1950   owner W. McKay Sandend
Loa.ft / m 69ft / 21.m   Brth ft / m 18ft / 5.4m   Dpth ft / m 9.6ft / 2.92m
Engine Hp / kw 152hp / 113kw Gardner
History 1970's sold for a wild life survey vessel

CARONIA   INS 146
Yard No 125   year 1953   owner J.Campbell Lossiemouth
Loa.ft / m 69ft / 21.3m   Brth ft / m 18.2ft / 5.5m   Dpth ft / m 7.9ft / 2.4m
Engine Hp / kw   152hp / 113kw Gardner
History 1976 Ben Aigen INS 146, 1980 no record in Olsens Almanac

ESTROLITA   BCK 6

Yard No128   year 1954 (Peterhead)   owner W.B.Herd Findochty
Loa.ft / m 73ft / 22.2m   Brth ft / m 19ft / 5.9m   Dpth ft / m 9.3ft / 2.83m
Engine Hp / kw   152hp / 113kw Gardner
History 1964 D 225, 2002 no record found in Almanac

GREEN PASTURES   BF 4

Yard No 131   year   1954   owner   J.Gardiner, /W Wilson Portknockie
Loa.ft / m 39.9ft / 12.1m   Brth ft / m 14.9ft / 4.5m   Dpth ft / m 6.8ft / 2.07m
Engine Hp / kw   66hp /49 kw Kelvin
History 1960's Provider LH 435, 1968 TT18, 1971 work boat based Gourock

HARVEST HOPE   PD 120

Yard No 132   year 1954 (Peterhead)   owner   R.W.Stephen Boddam
Loa.ft / m 39.9ft / 12.1m   Brth ft / m 14.9ft / 4.54m   Dpth ft / m 6.8ft / 2.07m
Engine Hp / kw   66hp / 49kw Kelvin
History 1969 Tern CN12, 1980 FY registered,1983 Jeanie Marie RX 328

HMS GREETHAM   M 2632

Yard No123   year 1955   owner   Admiralty
Loa.ft / m 110ft / 33.5 m   Brth ft / m 21.2 ft / 6.5 m   Dpth ft / m 5.5ft / 1.7 m
Engine Hp / kw   twin 1,100hp / 82 kw Paxman
History 1962 sold to Libya renamed **ZUARA,** 1973 Broken up

HMS Greetham on her sea trials

HMS MONKTON   M 1155
Yard No 124   year 1955   owner   Admiralty
Loa.ft / m   158ft / 42.7m   Brth ft / m 28.8ft / 8.8m Dpth ft / m 8.2ft / 2.5m
Engine Hp / kw 3000hp / 2237kw Mirrilees
History 1971 P1055 re designed for Patrol Squadron Hong Kong
28-4-72 arrived Hong Kong.   4-85 broken up at Hong Kong

HMS WOOLASTON   M 1194
Yard No 126   year 1955   owner   Admiralty
Loa.ft / m 158ft / 42.7m   Brth ft / m 28.8ft / 8.8m   Dpth ft / m 8.2ft / 2.5m
Engine Hp / kw   3000hp / 2237kw Mirrilees
History 29-4-69 Thames, 1975 Woolaston 1-81 broken up Sittingbourne

H M S LEWISTON   M 1208

Yard No 144   year 1959   owner   Admiralty
Loa.ft / m 153ft / 46.6m   Brth ft / m 28.3ft / 8.6m   Dpth ft / m 14.9ft / 4.5m
Engine Hp / kw 3000hp / 2237kw Mirrlees
History 1986 became target ship in Aberforth missile range Wales

MOYNESS   INS 124
Yard No 146   year 1956   owner   M. McIntosh Nairn
Loa.ft / m 66.5ft / 20.2 m Brth ft / m   18.9ft / 5.7 m Dpth ft / m 9.6ft / 2.6m
Engine Hp / kw   152hp / 113kw Gardner
History 1970 PL 12, 1976 W 86

LOCH KILDONAN   A 84
Yard No 141   year 1956   owner W.Stewart Aberdeen
Loa.ft / m 100.8ft / 30.7m   Brth ft / m 22ft / 6.7m   Dpth ft / m 11ft / 3.35m
Engine Hp / kw 335hp / 249 kw Ruston
History 1970 PD 79, 17th January 1987 sank

STAR OF LORETTO   A 186
Yard No 155   year 1958   owner Walker Steam Fishing Co Aberdeen
Loa.ft / m 130ft / 39.6m   Brth ft / m 25ft / 7.6m   Dpth ft / m 12.9ft / 3.9m
Engine Hp / kw   642hp / 478kw Widdop
History 1964 Admiral Mountbatten, 1979 no record in Olsens Almanac

Star of Loretto on Trials

EFFULGENCE   BF 24
Yard No 134   year   1955   owner   J.Gardiner Cullen
Loa.ft / m 51.3ft / 15.6m   Brth ft / m 16ft / 4.8m   Dpth ft / m 7.1ft / 2.1m
Engine Hp / kw   95hp / 70kw Gardner
History 1963 Silver Cord II BCK 200, 1976 AH 70, 1993 sold for Pleasure craft

SUILVEN   BF 33
Yard No 140   year 1955   owner J.Cowie Portknockie
Loa.ft / m 51.3ft / 15.3m Brth ft / m 16ft / 4.8m   Dpth ft / m 7.1ft / 2.1m
Engine Hp / kw 95hp / 70kw Gardner
History 1974 Craigenroan BCK 93, 1975/76 sank off Mallaig

GREEN PASTURES   N 20
Yard No 133   year 1955   owner   V. Chambers Annalong
Loa.ft / m 69.8ft / 21.2m   Brth ft / m 19.7ft / 6m   Dpth ft / m 9.6ft / 2.9m
Engine Hp / kw   152hp / 113kw Gardner
History 1966 sold to New Zealand

GREEN ISLE   N 256
Yard No 177   year 1959   owner   V. Chambers Annalong
Loa.ft / m 73ft / 22.2m   Brth ft / m 20.4ft / 6.2m Dpth ft / m 9.3ft / 2.8m
Engine Hp / kw   152hp 113kw Gardner
History 1974 D 52, 1997 no record found in Almanac

SEALGAIR   WK 241
Yard No 127   year 1954   owner M.McKay Lairg
Loa.ft / m 66.1ft / 20.1m Brth ft / m 18.3ft / 5.5m Dpth ft / m 6.7ft / 2.07m
Engine Hp / kw 152hp / 113kw Gardner
History -first boat from the H & M Yard at Peterhead.
1973 sold Ireland W 241, 2002 no record in the Almanac

KYANA   GY 232
Yard No 147   year 1956   owner   V.Nielson Grimsby
Loa.ft / m 65.1ft / 19.8m Brth ft / m 18ft / 5.4m Dpth ft / m 8.9ft / 2.7m
Engine Hp / kw   152hp /113kw Gardner
History 1961 sank in a North Sea Gale

First Danish Seine Netter

SUSITNA   GY 113

Yard No 136   year 1955 (Peterhead)   owner V.Nielson Grimsby
Loa.ft / m 65.1ft / 19.8m Brth ft / m 18ft / 5.4m Dpth ft / m 8.9ft / 2.7m
Engine Hp / kw   152hp / 113kw Gardner
History 1993 Decommissioned

NORDBORG   H 35
Yard No 151   year   1957   owner St Andrew Fishing Co Hull
Loa.ft / m 65.1ft / 19.84 m   Brth ft / m   18ft / 5.48 m   Dpth ft / m 8.9ft / 2.71 m
Engine Hp / kw   152hp / 113 kw
History 1988 Mourne Endeavour N 235, 1996 Decommissioned

LING BANK   GY 426
Yard No 153   year   1957   owner Delga Fishing Co Grimsby
Loa.ft / m 63.1ft / 19.23m   Brth ft / m   17.6ft / 5.36 m   Dpth ft / m 9.1ft / 2.77m
Engine Hp / kw   105hp / 78 kw Paxman
1993 no record in Olsens almanac

Launch of Ling Bank GY 426

SAXON II   GY 499
Yard No 160   year 1958   owner Forward Fishing Co Grimsby
Loa.ft / m 65.1ft / 19.7m   Brth ft / m 18.9ft / 5.7m   Dpth ft / m 8.9ft / 2.7m
Engine Hp / kw   152hp / 113 kw
History 1980 Peacewave GY 499, 1980 Sank in the North sea

SAXON KING   GY 629
Yard No 168   year   1959   owner   L.Sorensen Grimsby
Loa.ft / m65.1ft / 19.7m   Brth ft / m 18.9ft / 5.7m Dpth ft / m 8.9ft / 2.7m
Engine Hp / kw   152hp /113kw Gardner
History 1980- Delvan GT 629, 1995 no record in Almanac

BINKS   GY 617
Yard No 178   year 1959   owner Loumand Fishing Co Grimsby
Loa.ft / m 58ft / 17.6m Brth ft / m 15.10ft / 4.60m Dpth ft / m 9.6ft / 2.9m
Engine Hp / kw 114hp / 85 kw Gardner
History 1996 Scrapped

WHITE BANK   GY 620

Yard No 179   year 1960   owner Delga Fishing Co Grimsby
Loa.ft / m 58ft / 17.6m   Brth ft / m 16.4ft / 5.02m   Dpth ft / m 9.6ft / 2.9m
Engine Hp / kw   133hp / 99kw Paxman
History 1990 no record in Almanac

ADORIAM   PD 158

Yard No 145   year 1956   owner   A. Strachan Peterhead
Loa.ft / m 39.9ft / 12.1 m   Brth ft / m 15.3ft / 4.6 m   Dpth ft / m 5.7ft / 1.7m
Engine Hp / kw   66hp / 49 kw   Kelvin
History later Starlight LK 366, 1980's A 47, 1999 based Ireland, 2005 Houseboat

STRATHDOON   BA 122
Yard No 181   year   1960 owner A. Smith Ayr
Loa.ft / m 39.8ft / 12.1m   Brth ft / m 14.9ft / 4.5 m Dpth ft / m 6.3ft / 1.9 m
Engine Hp / kw   94hp / 70 kw Gardner
History 1973 Boy David TT78, 1996 scrapped Carradale Argyll

LIBERTY   INS 154
Yard No 154   year 1956   owner   G.Young Hopeman
Loa.ft / m 66.5ft / 20.2m   Brth ft / m 18.9ft / 5.7m Dpth ft / m 9.6ft / 2.9m
Engine Hp / kw   152hp /113kw Gardner
History 1979 B 282, 2001 Decommissioned

OPPORTUNE II   BCK 60

Yard No 157   year 1956   owner   G.Murray Buckie
Loa.ft / m 70.4ft / 21.4m   Brth ft / m 20.01ft / 6.1m   Dpth ft / m 6.5ft . 2.01m
Engine Hp / kw   152hp / 113 kw Gardner
History 1973 Saffron INS 95, ---2000 various owners 2001 Decommissioned

FRAGRANT ROSE   BCK 64

Yard No 158   year 1957   owner W.J.Smith Portessie
Loa.ft / m72.2ft / 22m   Brth ft / m 19.8ft / 6m   Dpth ft / m 6.6ft / 2.04m
Engine Hp / kw   152hp / 113kw Gardner
History 1971 B 74, 1997 various owners, 1997 Mary Elspeth FR 900, 2002 no record

CALEDONIA   INS 311
Yard No 142   year 1956   owner J.C.Thomson Lossiemouth
Loa.ft / m 69.9ft / 21.3m   Brth ft / m 19.7ft / 6.1m Dpth ft / m 9.6ft / 2.6m
Engine Hp / kw   152hp / 113 kw Gardner
History 1969 Caledonian Rose D 331, 2006 Scrapped

YUKON STAR   BCK 98
Yard No 172   year 1959   owner V.Nielson Grimsby
Loa.ft / m 72.8ft / 22.1m   Brth ft / m 19.1ft / 5.8m Dpth ft / m 9.6ft / 2.9m
Engine Hp / kw   240hp / 178kw Kelvin
History 1964 Athabasca FD 242,1974 GY 288,1985 Our Vanclare GY 288 1995 scrapped

YUKON FISHER   BCK 107
Yard No 175   year 1959   owner V. Nielsen Grimsby
Loa.ft / m 73ft / 22.2m   Brth ft / m 20.4ft / 6.2m   Dpth ft / m 9.6ft / 2.9m
Engine Hp / kw   240hp / 178 kw Kelvin
History 1964 Matanuska FD 243, 1971 GY 243, 1973 sank North Sea

DREADNOUGHT   A 377
Yard No 174   year 1959   owner Grampian Fishing Co Aberdeen
Loa.ft / m 102.4ft / 31.08m   Brth ft / m 22ft / 6.7m   Dpth ft / m 11ft / 3.3m
Engine Hp / kw   454hp / 338 kw Ruston
History 1970 based Lowestoft, 1975 Putford Harrier stand by vessel, 2000 sold

BROADHAVEN   A 479

Yard No 173   year   1959   owner   Faithlie Fishing Co Aberdeen
Loa.ft / m 102ft / 31m   Brth ft / m   22ft / 6.7m   Dpth ft / m 11ft / 3.3m
Engine Hp / kw   454hp / 338 kw Ruston
History 1972 sold, no record in Almanac

OCEAN VENTURE   BF 263
Yard No 191   year 1962   owner J.Watt Gardenstown
Loa.ft / m 45.5ft / 13.8m   Brth ft / m 15.2ft / 4.6m   Dpth ft / m 6.3ft / 1.9m
Engine Hp / kw   84hp / 62kw Gardner

History 1974 Sincerity AH 58, 1983 LH 188,

The First Yacht built at the Yard in Buckie

KYTRA

Yard No 171   year 1960   owner G.Goodsbody Inverness
Loa.ft / m 56ft / 17m   Brth ft / m 16ft / 4.8m Dpth ft / m 9.2ft / 2.8m
Engine Hp / kw   Gardner
History 1980's American owner based at Troon,

ANDVARI
Yard No 184   year 1960   owner J.MacKenzie Fochabers
Loa.ft / m 47.1ft / 14.3m   Brth ft / m   Dpth ft / m
Engine Hp / kw
History 2006 seen lying in the mud at Falmouth
(Apparently fell off whilst lying at the quay and staved in her side)

ASTRA VOLANTE
Yard No 194   year   1961   owner Sir John Grady
Loa.ft / m 56ft / 17m   Brth ft / m 16ft / 4.8m   Dpth ft / m 9.2ft / 2.8m
Engine Hp / kw   158hp / 117 kw Gardner
History later renamed **LEONOR II** based Barcelona

ARVOR III
Yard No 196   year 1962   owner Francois Ouvre, Paris
Loa.ft / m 63ft / 19.2m   Brth ft / m 17.9ft / 5.4m   Dpth ft / m 10.4ft / 3.1m
Engine Hp / kw   254hp / 189 kw Gardner
History 1995: owner Mark Tyler Sheldon, Maine, New England. USA

FERRARA
Yard No 197   year 1963   owner Mr D. Crudsen Faringdon
Loa.ft / m 65ft / 19.8m   Brth ft / m 16ft / 4.8m   Dpth ft / m 10ft / 3.04m
Engine Hp / kw   254hp / 189 kw Twin Gardners

SCOTTISH SIMO

Yard No 198   year 1962   owner   Wing Commander Spier, Nairn
Loa.ft / m 44.2ft / 13.4m   Brth ft / m 14.8ft / 4.51m   Dpth ft / m 7ft / 2.1m
Engine Hp / kw

MARANDI

Yard No 249   year 1973   owner J.H. MacKenzie Fochabers
Loa.ft / m 63ft / 19.2m   Brth ft / m 19.1ft / 5.8 m   Dpth ft / m 9.3ft / 2.8 m
Engine Hp / kw   twin 176hp / 131 kw Gardners

EDINDOUNE   BCK 142
Yard No 189   year 1960   owner John H.MacKenzie Buckie
Loa.ft / m37ft / 11.2m   Engine Hp / kw 58hp / 43 kw Perkins
History 1980's Horizon SY 294, 1990 based Connel near Oban

SOLOMON ISLANDS FERRY

CORAL PRINCESS
Yard No 188   year 1961   owner   Solomon Islands Council
Loa.ft / m89.3ft / 27.2m   Brth ft / m 21ft / 6.4m Dpth ft / m 11ft / 3.3m
Engine Hp / kw   300hp / 223 kw Twin Gardners

ADEN FISHERY RESEARCH VESSEL

RIZQ - AL - BAHR   A 73
Yard No 206   year 1964   owner Dept. of Fisheries Aden
Loa.ft / m67ft / 20.4m   Brth ft / m 20.4ft / 6.2m Dpth ft / m 10.6ft / 3.2m
Engine Hp / kw   320hp / 238 kw Kelvin

VILLAGE MAID   CT 51
Yard No 195   year 1961   owner W.C.Watterson Isle of Man
Loa.ft / m 50ft / 15.2m   Brth ft / m 17.6ft / 5.2m   Dpth ft / m 7.3ft / 2.2m
Engine Hp / kw   150hp 111kw Gardner
History 1973 sold to Ireland SO 315

ARDELLE   BCK 227
Yard No 207   year 1964   owner   W.B.Herd Findochty
Loa.ft / m 74.5ft / 22.7m   Brth ft / m 22.3ft / 6.8m   Dpth ft / m 9ft / 2.7m
Engine Hp / kw 501hp / 369 kw Mercedes
History 1976-2002 various owners - 2002 Scrapped at Macduff

COVESEA   INS 307
Yard No 210   year 1965   owner J.Campbell Lossiemouth
Loa.ft / m62.6ft / 19m   Brth ft / m 18.5ft / 5.6m   Dpth ft / m 8ft / 2.4m
Engine Hp / kw 200hp / 149 kw Gardner
History 1976 Shannon IV, 1986 Shannon C N 307, 1989 Mark A INS 137, 1991 Valour B 289, 1996 D 476,
2000 no record

GOLDEN STRAND   BF 403

Yard No 211   year 1966   owner: Cecil Mair Cullen
Loa.ft / m 50ft / 15.2m   Brth ft / m   15.7ft / 4.7m Dpth ft / m 7.6ft / 2.3m
Engine Hp / kw   180hp / 134 kw Caterpillar
History 1974 SY 173, 1977 / 1980 Seljefisk H-5-0 1985 Kystifisk H-5-0 1990 TK-19-K

FALCON   INS 235

Yard No 203   year   1963   owner J.Sutherland Hopeman
Loa.ft / m59.9ft / 18.2m   Brth ft / m 18.3ft / 5.5m   Dpth ft / m 7.3ft / 2.2m
Engine Hp / kw   150hp / 111kw Gardner
History 1974 Favour INS 235, 1994 scrapped

FLOURISH II   INS 123

Yard No 213   year 1966   owner   J.M.Sutherland, Hopeman
Loa.ft / m 61.6ft / 18.7m   Brth ft / m 18.4ft / 5.6m Dpth ft / m 7.8ft / 2.3m
Engine Hp / kw   200hp / 149kw Gardner
History 1992 N 123, 1994 Scrapped

FAIR MORN   BA 295

Yard No 215   year 1966   owner A.Munro Ayr
Loa.ft / m 61.6ft / 18.7m   Brth ft / m 18.4ft / 5.6m Dpth ft / m 7.8ft / 2.3m
Engine Hp / kw   200hp / 149 kw Caterpillar
History 1983 Anna Bhan INS 319, 1994 scrapped at Dundee

NEW DAWN   BA 18
Yard No 225   year 1968   owner J.S.Munro Ayr
Loa.ft / m 64.9ft / 19.7m   Brth ft / m 19ft / 5.7m Dpth ft / m 8.1ft / 2.4m
Engine Hp / kw 345hp / 257kw Caterpillar
History 2002 scrapped Loch Ryan

GREEN PASTURES II   N 210
Yard No 209   year 1965   owner   V.Chambers Annalong
Loa.ft / m 74.1ft / 22.5m   Brth ft / m 22.2ft / 6.7m Dpth ft / m 9.6ft / 2.9m
Engine Hp / kw   380hp / 283kw Caterpillar
History 1988-----2002 various owners 2002 sold out of fishing

COMET III   BCK 242
Yard No 217   year 1967   owner: R.Phimister Buckie
Loa.ft / m 74.9ft / 22.8m   Brth ft / m 20.4ft / 6.2m   Dpth ft / m 7.2ft / 2.2m
Engine Hp / kw   395hp / 295 Mercedes
History 1971 Arcturus, 1976 Marina, 1994 Confide BF 324 1999 sold out of fishing

JANEEN   BCK 5
Yard No 218   year 1968   owner: J. Smith Buckie
Loa.ft / m 50ft / 15.2 m   Brth ft / m 15.9ft / 4.8 m   Dpth ft / m 6.2ft / 1.8 m
Engine Hp / kw 210hp / 156 kw Caterpillar
History 1975 LK 277, 1980 A 677, 1986 N 91, 1988 LO 81

HELENA   BCK 248
Yard No 220   year 1967   owner: J.Strachan Portessie
Loa.ft / m71.7ft / 21.8m   Brth ft / m 20.3ft / 6.18m Dpth ft / m 8.8ft / 2.6m
Engine Hp / kw   200hp /149kw Gardner
History: 1976 Marlene, 1981 Aquarius INS 286, 1994 scrapped

SEAFIRE   UL 260
Yard No 221   year 1967   owner: J.Main Nairn
Loa.ft / m 63.3ft / 19.2m   Brth ft / m 19.3ft / 5.8m Dpth ft / m 8.6ft / 2.6m
Engine Hp / kw   180hp / 134 kw Caterpillar
History: 1977 Freedom III BA 280

AJAX   INS 168
Yard No 223   year 1968   owner: W. Campbell Lossiemouth
Loa.ft / m 77.5ft / 23.5m   Brth ft / m 22.4ft / 6.8m Dpth ft / m 9.9ft / 3.02m
Engine Hp / kw   380hp / 283 kw Caterpillar.   History: 1973 Harvest Hope PD 96,
1976 Star of Bethlehem, 1987 Opportunus, 1995 Benaiah III N 841

HORIZON   INS 21
Yard No 228   year 1969   owner J. Thomson Lossiemouth
Loa.ft / m 78ft / 23.7m   Brth ft / m 22.3ft / 6.7m   Dpth ft / m 9.8ft / 2.9m
Engine Hp / kw 400hp / 298 kw Caterpillar
History 1979 BCK 212, 1988 FR 261, 1996 Scrapped

HEATHERY BRAE   BF 26
Yard No 230   year 1969   owner A.Innes Portknockie
Loa.ft / m 54.3ft / 16.5m   Brth ft / m 17.3ft / 5.3m   Dpth ft / m 6.5ft / 1.9m
Engine Hp / kw   172hp / 128 kw Gardner
History 1988 Kildonan UL 145

MONADHLIATH   INS 140
Yard No 227   year 1968   owner: A.Jack Avoch
Loa.ft / m 59.6ft / 18.6m   Brth ft / m 19ft / 5.7m   Dpth ft / m 8.6ft / 2.6m
Engine Hp / kw   200hp / 149 Gardner
History: 1970 sank after calor gas explosion in the Minch

MONADHLIATH   INS 140
Yard No 238   year 1971   owner   A.Jack Avoch
Loa.ft / m 63.5ft / 19.3m   Brth ft / m 19.2ft / 5.8m Dpth ft / m 6.88ft / 2.1m
Engine Hp / kw   200hp / 149 Gardner
History 2002 converted to houseboat for German owner based Strande

OLBEK   GY 1389
Yard No 219   year 1967   owner L. Sorenson Grimsby
Loa.ft / m 65.1ft / 19.8m   Brth ft / m 18.5ft / 5.6m Dpth ft / m 6.9ft / 2.1m
Engine Hp / kw   200hp / 149 kw Gardner
History 2004 scrapped

PACEMAKER   GY 165
Yard No 231   year 1970   owner Delga Fishing Co Grimsby
Loa.ft / m 54.4ft / 16.6m   Brth ft / m 17.5ft / 5.3m Dpth ft / m 6.2ft / 1.9m
Engine Hp / kw   150hp / 111 kw Gardner
History 1986---2004 various owners 2004 based Devon

MINERVA   BCK 24
Yard No 232   year 1970   owner: A.McKay Buckie
Loa.ft / m 71ft / 21.6m   Brth ft / m 21ft / 6.2m   Dpth ft / m 8ft / 2.3m
Engine Hp / kw   230hp / 171 kw Gardner
History 1986 FR 147, 1988 Margaret Anne INS 130, 1997 Osprey, 2003 scrapped

SCARLET LINE   LH 55
Yard No 233   year   1970   owner: G.Buchanan Port Seton
Loa.ft / m 77ft / 23.4m   Brth ft / m 22.4ft / 6.8m   Dpth ft / m 9.6ft / 2.9m
Engine Hp / kw   400hp / 298 kw   Kelvin
History 1986 Charisma FR 75, 1998 G 220, 2005 no record found in Almanac

SUNRISE   UL 66
Yard No 229   year   1969   owner J.Campbell Lossiemouth
Loa.ft / m 65ft / 19.8m   Brth ft / m 19.3ft / 5.8m   Dpth ft / m 7.3ft / 2.2m
Engine Hp / kw   200hp / 149kw Gardner
History 1980's wrecked on the West Coast

ALKAID   INS 102
Yard No 234   year   1970   owner   G.S.Main Hopeman
Loa.ft / m64.9ft / 19.8m   Brth ft / m 19.4ft / 5.9m   Dpth ft / m 6.8ft / 2.09m
Engine Hp / kw   230hp /171 kw   Gardner
History 1983 Alvidra WK 111, 1996 Strathdonnan, 1997 Rhodonna B 14

Launch of Seaforth BCK 177

SEAFORTH   BCK 177
Yard No 236   year 1971   owner   D.Flett, Findochty
Loa.ft / m 72.2ft / 22.3m   Brth ft / m 21.3ft / 6.5m   Dpth ft / m 7.6ft / 2.3m
Engine Hp / kw   375hp / 279 kw Caterpillar
History: 1987 Amity PD 177, 1997 sold to Ireland S 233

Launch of Seagull BF 74

SEAGULL   **BF 74**
Yard No 239   year   1971   owner   K.West Macduff
Loa.ft / m 55.3ft / 16.7m   Brth ft / m 18.3ft / 5.5m   Dpth ft / m 6.9ft / 2.01m
Engine Hp / kw   365hp / 272 kw Caterpillar
History: 1982 DA 3, 1987 BCK 62, 2001 Sustain BCK 62,

THE LAUNCH OF THE SAILING SCHOONER CAPTAIN SCOTT

CAPTAIN SCOTT

CAPTAIN SCOTT
UNDER SAIL

CAPTAIN SCOTT
Yard No 235   year 1971   owner   Dulverton Trust
Loa.ft / m 144.3ft / 43.9m   Brth ft / m 28ft / 8.5m   Dpth ft / m
Engine Hp / kw   460hp / 343 kw Twin 230hp Gardners
History later sold to Oman renamed Shabab Oman (Youth of Oman)

UNITY   BCK 57
Yard No 240   year 1972   owner   J.Flett Buckie
Loa.ft / m 55.6ft / 16.9m   Brth ft / m 18.5ft / 5.6m   Dpth ft / m 6.9ft / 2.1m
Engine Hp / kw   325hp / 242 kw Caterpillar
History: 1986 Silver Star FR 73, 1988 BCK 131, 2002 Scrapped

CELNIUS   BCK 151
Yard No 245   year 1972   owner: W.J.Mair Buckie
Loa.ft / m 55.6ft / 16.9m   Brth ft / m 18.6ft / 5.6m   Dpth ft / m 6.9ft / 2.1m
Engine Hp / kw   328hp / 245 kw Caterpillar
History: 1987 Tenacious BCK 119, 1993 Dalriada BCK 180, 1998 Sarah Joan LK 987, 2004 scrapped

GOLDEN SPLENDOUR   INS 63
Yard No 244   year 1973   owner: T.Ross Burghead
Loa.ft / m 79.9ft / 24.3m   Brth ft / m 23.4ft / 7.1m   Dpth ft / m 8.2ft / 2.5m
Engine Hp / kw   500hp / 372 kw, Alpha
History 1973-----1997 various owners, 1997 sold to Ireland G 222, 2002 no record

OCEAN TRUST   BF 307
Yard No 246   year   1973   owner J.Watt Gardenstown
Loa.ft / m 74ft / 22.4m   Brth ft / m 22ft / 6.6m   Dpth ft / m 7.5ft / 2.2m
Engine Hp / kw   575hp / 428 British Polar
History 1986 sold to Sweden , Ostanvag, 2001Vingasand SM 154, 2002 Rio LL 775,

SILVER SPRAY   BCK 87
Yard No 243   year 1973   owner: W.Flett Buckie
Loa.ft / m 55.9ft / 16.9m   Brth ft / m 18.7ft / 5.6m   Dpth ft / m 5.6ft / 1.71m
Engine Hp / kw   319hp / 238 kw Volvo
History: 1983 KY 154, 1989Ajax AH 32, 1990 based St Ives Cornwall

LAURISA   BA 145
Yard No 247   year 1973   owner   J.H. Gibson Maidens
Loa.ft / m 56ft / 17m   Brth ft / m 18.6ft / 5.6m   Dpth ft / m 5.7ft / 1.76m
Engine Hp / kw   230hp / 171 kw Gardner
History 1981 Green Brae INS 208,

MARGARITA   BF 32
Yard No 252   year   1974   owner   L. Mair Buckie
Loa.ft / m 74.8ft / 22.7m   Brth ft / m 21.2ft / 6.4m   Dpth ft / m 7.4ft / 2.2m
Engine Hp / kw   425hp / 317 kw Caterpillar
History 1992 Atlantic Star PD 322, 1997 scrapped Ireland

COPIOUS   BF 237
Yard No 257   year   1975   owner: W. McKay Portsoy
Loa.ft / m 74.7ft / 22.6m   Brth ft / m 21.3ft / 6.4m   Dpth ft / m 7.5ft / 2.2m
Engine Hp / kw   500hp / 372 kw Kelvin
History: 1995 Opportunus PD 96, 2002 scrapped Denmark

ARNBORG   H 272
Yard No 254   year 1974   owner Boston Deep Sea Fisheries Hull
Loa.ft / m 53.2ft / 16.1m   Brth ft / m 17.7ft / 5.3m Dpth ft / m 6.6ft / 2.06m
Engine Hp / kw   150hp / 111 kw Gardner
History 1980-1999 various owners, 1999 LK 172, 2006 based Portree Isle of Skye

VIKINGBORG   H 285
Yard No 255   year 1974   owner Boston Deep Sea Fisheries Hull
Loa.ft / m 53.3ft / 16.1m   Brth ft / m 17.6ft /5.35m Dpth ft / m 6.6ft / 2.02m
Engine Hp / kw   150hp / 111 kw Gardner
History 1980- 2005 various owners, 2005 owner W. Simmonds Mallaig.

Morning Star original build and afterwards with shelter deck fitted

MORNING STAR   BCK 10
Yard No 251   year 1974   owner: Cecil Mair Cullen
Loa.ft / m 55.4ft / 16.7m   Brth ft / m 18.7ft / 5.6m   Dpth ft / m 6.2ft / 1.89m
Engine Hp / kw   335hp / 249 kw Caterpillar
History 1995 based Aberdeen, 2004 scrapped Denmark

MORNING STAR   BCK 10
Yard No 251   year 1974   owner Cecil Mair Cullen
Loa.ft / m 55.4ft / 16.7m   Brth ft / m 18.7ft / 5.6m   Dpth ft / m 6.2ft / 1.89m
Engine Hp / kw   335hp / 249 kw Caterpillar
History 1995 based Aberdeen, 2004 scrapped Denmark

HEATHER SPRIG   BCK 153

Yard No 259   year 1975   owner J. Smith Portessie
Loa.ft / m 55.3ft / 16.8m   Brth ft / m 18.7ft / 5.7m Dpth ft / m 5.9ft / 1.8m
Engine Hp / kw   280hp / 208 kw Kelvin
History: 1988 Kemarvin BF 4, 2006 WK 814.

JANEEN II   BCK 29

Yard No 260   year   1976   owner J. Smith Buckie
Loa.ft / m 55.6ft / 16.9m   Brth ft / m 18.3ft / 5.5m Dpth ft / m 5.6ft / 1.7m
Engine Hp / kw   375hp / 279 Caterpillar
History 2003 scrapped Denmark

MORAVIA   INS 86
Yard No 262   year 1975   owner J.C Thompson Lossiemouth
Loa.ft / m71.2ft / 21.7m   Brth ft / m 20 ft / 6.09 m Dpth ft / m 6.9ft / 2.10m
Engine Hp / kw   230hp / 171 kw Gardner
History-1981 Moray View, 1996 Heritage B 786.

HARMONY   INS 257

Yard No 271   year 1978   owner A. McPherson Hopeman
Loa.ft / m 74.2ft / 22.6m   Brth ft / m 21ft / 6.4m Dpth ft / m 7.4ft / 2.2m
Engine Hp / kw   500hp / 372 kw Kelvin
History 1995 sold to Ireland D 207

GREENFIELD   N 57

Yard No 265   year 1977   owner V.Chambers Annalong Ireland
Loa.ft / m87.2ft/26.52m   Brth ft / m 24.1ft / 7.35 Dpth ft / m 12.4 ft / 4.2m
Engine Hp / Kw 800hp / 596 kw Blackstone
History 1984 Gullaks H-26-FE, 1989 Brodrene Husevag, 1997 Gunnerson M-70-M
History- 2000 Nordnes AS M-60-G, 2000 Ronaldnes AS M-6-G

GREEN ISLE   N 64

Yard No 266   year   1977   owner V. Chambers Annalong Ireland
Loa.ft / m 87.2ft /26.52 m   Brth ft / m 24.1ft/ 7.35 m   Dpth ft / m 12.4ft / 4.2 m
Engine Hp / kw   800 hp / 596kw Blackstone
History 1984 Soloyvag M-112-F, 2003 no record in Norwegian Almanac

Launch of St Kilda INS 47

ST KILDA   INS 47
Yard No 268   year 1978   owner J.W.C.Thompson Lossiemouth
Loa.ft / m 78.7ft / 23.9m   Brth ft / m 23.7ft / 7.2m Dpth ft / m 10.1ft / 3.08m
Engine Hp / kw   725hp / 540 kw   Caterpillar
History 1993 Qui Vive FR 201, 1998 Dalriada BF 262, 2003 scrapped Denmark

ACCORD   FR 262
Yard No 270   year 1978   owner W. McKay Fraserburgh
Loa.ft / m 69ft / 21.03m   Brth ft / m 22.2ft / 6.7m Dpth ft / m 7ft / 2.01m
Engine Hp / kw   500hp / 372 kw Kelvin
History 1990 BCK 262, owner G. Wilson Cullen.

CRYSTAL SEA   LH 97

Yard No 272   year   1979   owner A.B. Johnston Port Seton
Loa.ft / m 54.9ft / 16.7m   Brth ft / m 18.5ft / 5.6m   Dpth ft / m 6.46ft / 1.97m
Engine Hp / kw   365hp / 272 Caterpillar
History 1997 Fraoch Ban LK 966, 15-8-99 sank off Shetland

COEL – NA – MARA   BF 352
Yard No 274   year   1979   owner A. Watt Gardenstown
Loa.ft / m 55.5ft / 16.9m   Brth ft / m 18.6ft / 5.6m   Dpth ft / m 5.7ft / 1.7m
Engine Hp / kw   365hp / 273 kw Caterpillar
History 1998 K 1003, 2005 Shekinah INS 155,

STAR AWARD   BF 407
Yard No 277   year   1980   owner   M. Slater Macduff
Loa.ft / m 56.3ft / 17.07m   Brth ft / m 18.4ft / 5.5m   Dpth ft / m 5.6ft / 1.7m
Engine Hp / kw   415hp / 310kw Kelvin
History 1986 AH 77, 2001 Star of Hope FR 200, 2005 based Portavogie
2007 Cathzelle B222

FLOURISH II   LK 450
Yard No 278   year   1980   owner   J. Kay Whalsay Shetland
Loa.ft / m 56.3ft / 17.07m   Brth ft / m 18.4ft / 5.5m   Dpth ft / m 5.4ft / 1.6m
Engine Hp / kw   290hp / 216 kw Volvo
History 1992 Heathery Brae IV BF 87, 1999Leandra, BF 87, 2001 Primrose II BF 87

Launch of Avoca BCK 294

AVOCA   BCK 294

Yard No 280   year 1981   owner D. Campbell Findochty
Loa.ft / m 75.3ft / 22.8m   Brth ft / m 21.5ft / 6.5m   Dpth ft / m 7.4ft / 2.2m
Engine Hp / kw   415hp / 309 kw Kelvin
History 2002 scrapped at Macduff

KELLY   BCK 303
Yard No 283   year   1982   owner Danbrit Fishing Co Grimsby
Loa.ft / m 59.9ft / 18.17m   Brth ft / m 20.7ft / 6.28m   Dpth ft / m 8.1ft / 2.47m
Engine Hp / kw   328hp /244 kw Volvo
History 1989-2005- Various owners, 2005 DS 7, 2006 BCK 625

HAZELMORE II   BCK 83
Yard No 284   year 1983   owner B. More Buckie
Loa.ft / m 75.9ft / 23.1m   Brth ft / m 21.1ft / 6.4m Dpth ft / m 7.4ft / 2.2m
Engine Hp / kw   495hp / 369kw Caterpillar
History 1991 Ocean Reward III, 1997 Aurora BF 812, January 1999 sank off Fraserburgh

PROVIDENCE   BF 422
Yard No 281   year   1982   owner   D.A. Watt Gardenstown
Loa.ft / m 59.7ft / 18.2m   Brth ft / m 20.9ft / 6.3m Dpth ft / m 7.7ft / 2.3m
Engine Hp / kw   470hp / 350 kw Cummins
History 1995 Headway BF 856, 1998 Seaway PD 319, 1999 Headway , 2002 BF 856

SILVER FERN   FR 416
Yard No 282   year   1982   owner A.G. Wiseman Fraserburgh
Loa.ft / m 59.1ft / 2.2m   Brth ft / m 20.6ft / 6.3m Dpth ft / m 8.1ft / 2.2m
Engine Hp / kw   495hp / 370 kw Kelvin

BUNILLIDH   WK 96
Yard No 285   year   1984   owner   D. Cowie Helmsdale
Loa.ft / m 63.5ft / 19.3m   Brth ft / m 22.1ft / 6.7m Dpth ft / m 8.2ft / 2.5m
Engine Hp / kw 400hp / 298 kw Caterpillar
History 1999 Achieve FR 100

LOCH INCHARD   UL 44
Yard No 287   year 1984   owner   J. MacKay Kinlochbervie
Loa.ft / m 60.1ft /18.3m   Brth ft / m 21.2ft/ 6.4m Dpth ft / m 7.6ft / 2.3m
Engine Hp / kw   360hp / 262 kw Volvo

PTARMIGAN   BCK 26
Yard No 288   year   1985   owner   D.A. Goodbrand Portsoy
Loa.ft / m 75.8ft / 23.1m   Brth ft / m 21.06ft / 6.4m   Dpth ft / m 7.4ft / 2.2m
Engine Hp / kw   495hp / 369 kw Kelvin
History 2000 Christine K. PD 306, 2003 scrapped Denmark

AQUILA II   BCK 43

Yard No 289   year   1986   owner E. Simpson Buckie
Loa.ft / m 65.5ft / 19.9m   Brth ft / m 22.1ft / 6.7m Dpth ft / m 8.05ft / 2.4m
Engine Hp / kw   400hp / 298 kw Caterpillar
History 1992 Chrisona BF 361, 1999 Bountiful BF 79

UNITY   BCK 35
Yard No 290   year   1986   owner J.Flett Buckie
Loa.ft / m 60.1ft / 18.2m   Brth ft / m 22.2ft / 6.7m Dpth ft / m 8.3ft / 2.5m
Engine Hp / kw   495hp / 369kw Caterpillar
History 1993 Caledonia BCK 35, 2007 Aubretia BCK 32

HOPE   BCK 59
Yard No 291   year   1986   owner L.G. McKay Buckie
Loa.ft / m 65ft / 19.8m   Brth ft / m 22.2ft / 6.7m Dpth ft / m 8.3ft / 2.5m
Engine Hp / kw   310hp / 295 kw Gardner
History 1998 FR 906, 2001 sank off Aberdeen

BONAVENTURE   LH 111
Yard No 292   year 1987   owner T.I. Bain Eyemouth
Loa.ft / m 71.2ft / 21.7m   Brth ft / m 22.1ft / 6.7m Dpth ft / m8.3ft / 2.5m
Engine Hp / kw   495hp / 369 kw Caterpillar
History 1994 owner Bryan Blackie Eyemouth

REBECCA   LH 11

Yard No 293   year 1987   owner R. Miller Musselburgh
Loa.ft / m 67.6ft / 20.6m   Brth ft / m 22.1ft / 6.7m   Dpth ft / m 7.9ft / 2.4m
Engine Hp / kw   495hp / 369 kw Caterpillar
History 1994 Heatherbelle VI LH 272, 1998 Rebecca LH 11.

ELEANDA   BCK 60
Yard No 294   year   1988   owner D. Main Buckie
Loa.ft / m 75.5ft / 23.03m   Brth ft / m 23.19ft / 7.07m Dpth ft / m 8ft / 2.44m
Engine Hp / kw   650hp / 484 kw Kelvin
History 1992 Kevella BF 364, 2000 sold to Ireland Atlantic Fisher T 116

GERMOUNT   K 970
Yard No 297   year   1989   owner J. Peace Rousay Orkney
Loa.ft / m 42.9ft / 13.1m   Brth ft / m 17.4ft / 5.3m   Dpth ft / m 10.3ft / 3.13m
Engine Hp / kw   230hp / 171 kw Cummins
History 2002 owner D. MacMillan Lochboisdale South Uist

STELIMAR   CY 163

Yard No 295   year   1988   owner D.F. Macrae Grimsay South Uist
Loa.ft / m 40.3ft / 12.2m   Brth ft / m 16.01ft / 4.88m   Dpth ft / m 6.6ft / 2.04m
Engine Hp / kw   182hp / 135 kw Gardner
History 2002 owner I. Johnston Grimsay South Uist

GUIDING LIGHT   CY 127

Yard No 296   year   1988   owner D. Stewart Grimsay South Uist
Loa.ft / m41.6ft / 12.7m   Brth ft / m 16.01ft / 4.88m Dpth ft / m 7 ft / 2.07m
Engine Hp / kw   182 hp 135 kw Gardner
History 1999 owner G.N. Kirkpatrick Longhope Orkney

AQUARIA   K 232

Yard No 299   year 1990   owner E. Sinclair Stromness Orkney
Loa.ft / m 51.1ft / 15.5m   Brth ft / m 17.4ft / 5.4m Dpth ft / m 10.3ft / 3.14m
Engine Hp / kw   374hp / 275 kw Gardner
History 1999 owner D. Stewart Grimsay South Uist

EGALITE   K 366

Yard No 3000   year 1993   owner N. Matheson Stromness Orkney
Loa.ft / m 49.1ft / 15.2m   Brth ft / m 17ft / 5.2m Dpth ft / m 8ft / 2.6m
Engine Hp / kw 250hp / 179 kw Cummins
History 1994 owner B. Sutherland Hopeman, 2004 Nordic Way FR 973 2006 based Barra

LAUREL   PL 6
Yard No 299   year   1990   owner G.R. Comber Peel Isle of Man
Loa.ft / m54.5ft / 16.5m Brth ft / m 18.5ft / 5.6m Dpth ft / m 10.4ft / 3.1m
Engine Hp / kw   310hp / 231 kw   Gardner
History 1998 KY 986, 2004 LK 227, 2005 CY 341

JULIE   BF 211
Yard No 301   year 19 91   owner I. McKay Findochty
Loa.ft / m 39.13ft / 11.86m   Brth ft / m 15.18ft / 4.60m Dpth ft / m 8.6ft / 2.6m
Engine Hp / kw   250hp / 187 kw Gardner
History 1995 Kelly Ann II OB 156,

The following photographs show various members of the workforce and of other events during its various stages as a shipyard.

Willie Stewart & George Sutherland

Alex John Wood

Bill Rennie & George Campbell – Fairing Frames to take outer planking. - George Campbell was selected for a course on the Captain Scott – not only did he assist in the building but had first hand knowledge of her in her natural environment.

George Thomson & Jimmy Cathcart

Arthur Malone & Eddie Smith

Arthur Malone

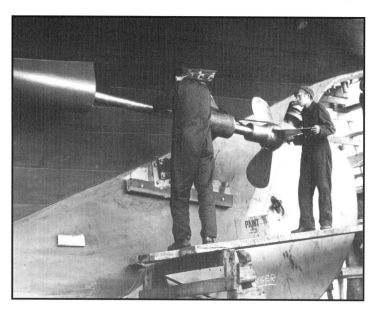

Dave Marshall engineer and David Taylor Apprentice engineer installing tail shafts on the Captain Scott

Alex Smith & Willie Robertson, drilling steel beams in preparation for lower decking

© The Buckie & District Fishing Heritage Centre Ltd.

Jim Farquhar & Alistair Muir

An aerial view of the yard

1982
Queen's visit to the Shipyard

Meeting the Queen and Prince Philip

Jim Farquhar shows the Queen round the yard

The Queen with Jim Farquhar departing from a visit to the fishing vessel Kelly

Duke of Edinburgh meeting the workforce

Alison Findlay presenting H.M. the Queen with a gift from the Shipyard

Appendix One

The complete list of ships built at Herd & Mackenzie Yards

Compiled by John Addison

No	Name	Reg No	Year	Dimensions (ft)	Power HP/KW	Tons
1	Bloomfield	BF 218	1906	83.7 x 18.0 x 8.6	16inch 27hp	83
2	Vallar Crown	BF 249	1906	82.40 x 18.00 x 8.50	16inch 26hp	78
3	Energy	BF 324	1906	85.1 x 18.0 x 8.50	16inch 20hp	79
4	Transit	BF 497	1907	85.20 x 18.0 x 8.6	16inch 31hp	83
5	Excelsior	BF 683	1907	86.10 x 18.10 x 8.70	16inch 30hp	85
6	Roxana	BF 831	1907	85.70 x 18.20 x 5.80	16inch 25hp	86
7	Petrel	BF 914	1907	86.00 x 18.30 x 18.30	16inch 30hp	86
8	Conie	BF 937	1907	85.30 x 18.30 x 8.80	16inch 30hp	85
9	Bonchief	BCK 17	1908	86.60 x 18.30 x 9.10	16inch 28hp	83
10	Desire	BCK 27	1908	86.70 x 18.30 x 9.10	16inch 30hp	83
11	Glen Albyne	BCK 53	1909	86.10 x 18.30 x 9.10	16inch 28hp	82
12	Sterlochy	BCK 65	1910	83.30 x 18.40 x 9.00	16inch 27hp	78
13	Docile III	BCK 70	1910	86.20 x 18.40 x 9.00	16inch 27hp	82
14	Home Friend	BCK 89	1911	87.80 x 18.60 x 9.10	16inch 24hp	89
15	Harvest Hope	BCK 90	1911	89.00 x 18.60 x 9.30	16inch 26hp	91
16	G S L	BCK 110	1912	88.60 x 18.80 x 9.30	16inch 29hp	85
17	David Flett	BCK 112	1912	87.90 x 18.90 x 9.20	16inch 29hp	84
18	Summerton	BCK 126	1912	87.40 x 19.10 x 9.20	16inch 29hp	83
19	Christina Craig	BK 271	1913	87.90 x 18.90 x 9.4	16inch 25hp	86
20	Maple Leaf		1913	37ft		
21	Monarda	PD 92	1913	89.80 x 18.90 x 9.1	16inch 29hp	89
22	Barley Rig	BCK 145	1914	87.80 x 19.20 x 9.10	16inch 35hp	88
23	Heather Sprig	BCK 153	1913	88.30 x 19.10 x 9.10	16inch 35hp	83
24	Lizzie Birrell	BCK 163	1913	91.20 x 19.20 x 9.50	16inch 35hp	92
25	Border King	BK 72	1914	90.60 x 19.20 x 9.40	18inch 31hp	92
26	Eglise	BCK 180	1914	92.60 x 19.10 x 9.60	16inch 30hp	99
27	Enterprising	BCK 187	1914	91.50 x 19.10 x 9.70	18inch 36hp	98
28	J & A	BK 304	1914	92.50 x 19.20 x 9.50	16inch 27hp	98
29	Elibank		1914			
30	Mary Swanston	BK 357	1916	93.20 x 19.30 x 9.60	16inch 44hp	109
31	Monarda	PD 266	1916	91.10 x 19.40 x 9.60	16inch 37hp	108
32	Obtain	BCK 355	1917	90.80 x 19.40 x 9.5	18inch 27hp	105
33	Solstice	HMS Drifter	1918	87.60 x 19.80 x 10.30	18inch 43hp	98
34	Silt	HMS Drifter	1918	87.60 x 19.80 x 10.30	18inch 43hp	
35	Sunspot	HMS Drifter	1920	87.60 x 19.80 x 10.30	18inch 34hp	100
36	Harvest Reaper	BCK 128	1925	87.00 x 19.10 x 9.8	16inch 29hp	98
37	Loranthus	BCK 3	1929	86.50 x 19.80 x 10.00	18inch 27hp	95
38	Nautilus	BCK 7	1929	65.00 x 18.50 x 8.60		
39	Lizzie West	LT 495	1930	90.60 x 20.00 x 9.50		
40	John Herd	FR 149	1931	91.90 x 20.10 x 9.90	18inch 43hp	103
41	Liberty	BF 429	1932	56.00 x 15.00 x 5.00		
42	Courage		1932	40.00 x 14.50		
43	Celerity	BCK 142	1933	56.00 x 16.00 x 6.00	54hp Gardner	

Owner	History
G & J S Flett Findochty	1915 / 1920 war service as Budleia, 1924 sold to Grimsby. 10/10/1926 - sank in North Sea
Farquhar, Cowie, Portessie	Scrapped 1949
George Mair Portknockie	1915 war service 1920 owner W Innes, 1938 scrapped
W. Ross Findochty	1915 war service 15/5/17 sunk off Fano island Adriatic
Duguid & Slater Portessie	1915 / 1920 war service 1929 reg BCK 53 1933 Scrapped
G. Smith Portessie	1913 Nexus BCK 159, 1915 war service 1918 mined Thames
W.Legge Findochty	1915 / 1919 war service 1936 scrapped
G.Herd Findochty	1915 / 1919 war service 1937 scrapped
A & G Herd Findochty	1916/1919 war service 1949 scrapped J.Cameron Peterhead
D.Smith Portessie	war service 1915/1919, & 1940/1944as Rosa, 1945 scrapped
W Burrell & J Herd Findochty	war service 1917/19, 1920FR 59, 1939 sunk in Loch Ewe
A G & W Flett Findochty	1916 / 19 war service 1947 PD 384 1948 scrapped
W & J Flett Findochty	1916 / 19 war service 1919 W.Findlay Cullen 1937 scrapped
J,W.Legge, J Flett Findochty	1915/20 warservice 1931 BF 257 A.McKay Sandend 1937
W Anderson Findochty	1915/20 war service 1925 BF 106 A Alexander 1937
A J & P Smith Portessie	1915/19 war service 1921 sold to Spain as Pareja Trawler
D. Flett Findochty	1916/19 war service 1925 Star of Light PD 167, 1931 FR 221, 1939/1946 war service 1950 scrapped
J & D Mair Portknockie	1915 / 1919 war service, 1925 sold to Buckie 1951 scrapped
R Cowe & Craig Eyemouth	1915 war service 15/2/18 sunk by enemy in the Dover Strait
Mr McKay Dunbeath	
C.B. & R.T Milne Peterhead	23rd June 1915 Sunk by Enemy Sub fishing East of Shetland
W & S Smith Buckie	27/8/14 mined and lost while fishing off the Tyne 5 crew lost
W.Smith & Phimister	war service 1917/20, & 1940/46 1952 sold for scrap
W B & R B Herd Findochty	war service 1916/20 & 1940/46 1946 sold to Norway
J & D Dougal Eyemouth	1919 sold to J Strachan Peterhead PD 158. 1946 Scrapped
W. Ross Findochty	1925 sold to P Buchan Cairnbulg FR 102 scrapped 1938
G.W.Smith Buckie	1918/19 war service 1924 INS 5, 1937 BK 63, 1940/45 War Service, 1945 FR26, 1947 SA 8, 1950 sold for scrap
T Lough & J Craig Eyemouth	1915 war service 4/4/1918 sunk, collision off Scarborough
J & J Sutherland Hopeman	
Peter Craig Eyemouth	1926 Dewy Eve BF 215, 1936 FR 269, 1940lost on war service
C.B. & R.T Milne Peterhead	1933 owner W Duthie, 1940 war service 8/11/41 sank Thames
Wm Findlay Cullen	1945 Rosevalley BF 80 1948 A/deen 1949 PD 22 1952 Scrap
Royal Navy	1920 Fishery Board 1921 INS 276, 1932 BF 140, 1949 scrap
Royal Navy	1921 INS 317, 1938 Mary Johnston BF 15, 1951 scrapped
G. Anderson Findochty	1945 FR 34, 1950 Scrapped
G.A.Smith Portessie	1939/45 war service, 1945 BF 58 (J.Ritchie) 1951 scrap
G.A.Smith Portessie	30/11/41 lost on Naval service at Dunkirk
James West Gardenstown	
John Herd Fraserburgh	1941/45 war service 1946 BF 94 (Frank West) 1951 scrap
Addison Cullen	
A. Bruce Findochty	Later Converted to Houseboat in Holland

No	Name	Reg No	Year	Dimensions (ft)	Power HP/KW	Tons
42	Courage		1932	40.00 x 14.50		
43	Celerity	BCK 142	1933	56.00 x 16.00 x 6.00	54hp Gardner	
44	Covesea	INS 307	1933	56.00 x 16.00 x 6.00	54hp Gardner	22
45	Plough	INS 327	1934	58.00 x 16.30 x 5.90	54hp Gardner	25
46	Argosy	INS 11	1934	58.00 x 16.00 x 6.00	80hp National	33
47	Victory	INS 37	1934	58.00 x 16.00 x 7.80	54hp Gardner	33
48	Rosebud	INS 63	1934	58.00 x 16.00 x 7.80	80hp National	33
49	Olive leaf	INS 86	1934	60.00 16.60 x 6.60	72hp Gardner	30
50	Marguerite	INS 100	1934	56.00 x 16.60 x 6.60		
51	Anner		1934	58.00 x 16.60 x 6.60		
52	Comet		1935	58.00 x 16.60 x 6.60		
53	Fulmar	INS 252	1935	58.60 x 16.60 x 6.60		31
54	Kathleen	FRV	1935	55.00 x 16.00 x 8.00	60hp Glenniffer	
55	Silver Spray		1937	45.00 x 15.00 x 5.60	60hp Lister	
56	Quest	INS 297	1937	58.00 x 16.60 x 8.60		30
57	Larus	INS 312	1937	58.30 x 16.60 x 8.60	54hp Gardner	29
58	Harvest Hope	BCK 146	1938	65.00 x 17.60 x 8.60	72hp Gardner	41
59	Lochloy	INS 321	1938	55.00 x 16.60 x 8.60	54hp Gardner	29
60	Aderyn	Yacht	1938	42.00 x 14.30 x 6.00	50hp Mathers	
61	Jeannie MacKay	WK 316	1938	54.00 x 16.00 x 8.60	68hp Gardner	27
62	Athena	INS 334	1938	62.00 x 17.00 x 8.60	72hp Gardner	30
63	Ebeneezer	BCK 160	1939	55.00 x 17.00 x 8.60	85hp Gardner	31
64	Morning Star	INS 35	1939	61.00 x 17.00 x 7.00	85hp Gardner	
65	Oceanic	INS 71	1939	61.00 x 17.00 x 7.00	85hp Gardner	33
66	Whaler		1940	27.00 ft		
67	Whaler		1940	27.00 ft		
68	Whaler		1940	27.00 ft		
69	Whaler		1940	27.00 ft		
70	Dayspring		1941	60.00 x 17.10 x 7.30		
71	Whaler		1941	27.00 ft		
72	Whaler		1941	27.00 ft		
73	Whaler		1941	27.00 ft		
74	Whaler		1941	27.00 ft		
75	Minesweeper	MMS 4	1941	105 ft	Harland & Wolf	
76	Minesweeper	MMS 21	1941	105 ft	Harland & Wolf	
77	Minesweeper	MMS 53	1941	105 ft	Crossley	
78	Minesweeper	MMS 54	1941	105 ft	Crossley	
79	Minesweeper	MMS 192	1942	105 ft	National	
80	Minesweeper	MMS 193	1942	105 ft	National	
81	Minesweeper	MMS 211	1942	105 ft	Harland & Wolf	
82	Minesweeper	MMS 1015	1943	126 ft		
83	Minesweeper	MMS 1016	1943	126 ft		
84	Minesweeper	MMS 1047	1944	126 ft		

Owner   ## History

Owner	History
A. Bruce Findochty	Later Converted to Houseboat in Holland
Campbell Lossiemouth	
J. Flett Lossiemouth	1950'sBCK 152, 1957 b 102, 1967 LL 256, 1974 DO 58,
G.Campbell Lossiemouth	
Flett & Campbell Lossiemouth	
T Ross Burghead	
W&J Thomson Lossiemouth	
A.Campbell Lossiemouth	
J Murray Buckie	
Campbell Lossiemouth	
S Young Hopeman	
Scottish Fisheries Leith	1940/46 war service renamed Mildred 1946 Kathleen 1957 sold 1970s Kathleen Del Mar House boat in Tasmania
Lerwick	Good Shepherd ferry boat to Fair Isle
Barron Nairn	
A. Main Nairn	
Smith Buckie	1940's INS 67
A.Main Nairn	
Col. Hayes	
J.S. Mackay Helmsdale	
McPherson Hopeman	
J.Garden Portessie	1959 WK 135,1967 PD 45, 1977 converted based Fife 1978 renamed Barcadale based Loch Creran, Argyll
W&J Thomson Lossiemouth	
J.Main Burghead	1963 based Eyemouth, 1986 no record in Olsen's almanack
Admirality	
Admirality	
Admirality	
Admirality	
W&J Thomson Lossiemouth	
Admirality	
Admirality	
Admirality	
Admirality	
Admirality	1943 based Mediterranean. 1947 Scrapped
Admirality	1945 lent to France as D 241. 1948 broken up Brightlingsea
Admirality	1946-51 Greek Navy as Korytsa, 1-10-56 sold
Admirality	1946 sold Dutch Navy Hr Ms Marken II 1957 Dutch sea cadets
Admirality	1942 based Harwich, 1946 Salcombe. 1946 sold
Admirality	1944-46 118th MSF Normandy Invasion, 1957 Broken up
Admirality	1942 at Belfast, 1944 Harwich, 1945 Sheerness, 1946 Disposal
Admirality	1944 at Lowestoft, 1946 NW Europe, 25-10-46 sold
Admirality	at Leith, 1944 Portsmouth, 1945 DanishNavy, 1946 wrecked
Admirality	1944 at Leith, 22-11-46 sold

No	Name	Reg No	Year	Dimensions (ft)	Power HP/KW	Tons
85	75ft MFV	MFV 1043	1944	75.00 x 19.75 x 9.50	160hp Blackstone	50
86	75ft MFV	MFV 1044	1944	75.00 x 19.75 x 9.50	160hp Blackstone	50
87	75ft MFV	MFV 1045	1944	75.00 x 19.75 x 9.50	160hp Blackstone	50
88	75ft MFV	MFV 1087	1944	75.00 x 19.75 x 9.50	160hp Blackstone	50
89	45ft MFV	MFV 667	1944	49.75 x 15.25 x 5.75	60hp Atlantc	
90	45ft MFV	MFV 668	1944	49.75 x 15.25 x 5.75	60hp Atlantc	
91	75ft MFV	MFV 1046	1945	75.00 x 19.75 x 9.50	160hp Blackstone	50
92	75ft MFV	MFV 1088	1945	75.00 x 19.75 x 9.50	160hp Blackstone	50
93	75ft MFV	MFV 1151	1945	75.00 x 19.75 x 9.50	160hp Blackstone	50
94	75ft MFV	MFV 1152	1945	75.00 x 19.75 x 9.50	160hp Blackstone	50
95	75ft MFV	MFV1153	1945	75.00 x 19.75 x 9.50	160hp Blackstone	50
96	75ft MFV	MFV 1154	1946	75.00 x 19.75 x 9.50	160hp Blackstone	50
97	75ft MFV	MFV 1209	1946	75.00 x 19.75 x 9.50	160hp Blackstone	50
98	Guide On	INS 70	1946	62.00 x 17.70 x 7.70	114hp Gardner	36
99	Moravia	INS73	1946	68.00 x 19.60 x 8.60	152hp Gardner	44
100	Windermere	PD 203	1947	62.60 x 17.60 x 9.30	114hp Gardner	38
101	Arnhem	INS 117	1947	62.60 x 18.30 x 9.30	114hp Gardner	38
102	Orion	INS 125	1947	68.00 x 18.30 x 9.30	152hp Gardner	41
103	Corn Rig	INS 128	1947	62.00 x 18.00 x 9.30	114hp Gardner	39
104	Beechgrove	A 266	1947	75.00 x 19.00 x 9.90	206hp Ruston	58
105	Cedargrove	A 57	1947	75.00 x 19.00 x 9.90	206hp Ruston	55
106	Melita	INS 163	1947	65.00 x 18.00 x 9.60	160hp Blackstone	39
107	Incentive	INS 155	1948	62.00 x 18.00 x 9.30	114hp Gardner	34
108	Aureola	BCK 181	1948	65.00 x 18.00 x 9.60	120hp Blackstone	40
109	Souvenir	BCK 183	1948	67.00 x 18.00 x 9.60	160hp Blackstone	46
110	Acacia	BCK 184	1948	68.00 x 18.00 x 9.60	160hp Blackstone	46
111	Ocean Gleaner	INS 200	1948	62.00 x 18.00 x 9.30	114hp Gardner	34
112	Morayshire	INS 212	1948	62.00 x 18.00 x 9.30	114hp Gardner	34
113	Felicitous	A 620	1948	64.00 x 18.00 x 9.60	160hp Blackstone	40
114	Alliance	INS 242	1949	62.00 x 18.00 x 9.30	114hp Gardner	35
115	Reliant	INS 250	1949	65.00 x 18.00 x 9.60	120hp Blackstone	39
116	Devotion	INS 223	1949	65.00 x 18.00 x 9.60	114hp Gardner	38
117	Capella	BCK 11	1949	69.00 x 18.00 x 9.60	173hp Mirilees	40
118	Gladsome	BCK 77	1949	69.00 x 18.00 x 9.60	152hp Gardner	45
119	Caronia	INS 276	1950	65.00 x 18.00 x 9.60	152hp Gardner	39
120	Copious	BF 211	1950	69.00 x 18.00 x 9.60	152hp Gardner	45
121	HMS Cardinham	IMS 15	1953	110ft Minesweeper	Paxman	
122	HMS Chilcompton	CMS 22	1954	158ft Minesweeper	3,000hp Napier Deltic	
123	HMS Greetham	IMS 34	1955	110ft Minesweeper	Paxman	
124	HMS Monkton	CMS 55	1955	158ft Minesweeper	3,000hp Napier Deltic	
125	Caronia	INS 146	1953	69.00 x 18.00 x 9.60	152hp Gardner	49
126	HMS Woolaston	CMS 94	1955	158ft Minesweeper	3,000hp Napier Deltic	
127	Sealgair	WK 241	1954	65 x 17.8 x 9.1	152 / 113 Gardner	48

Owner	History
Admirality	1946 Kathleen Pirie A 207, 1947Fair Morn BF 340, 1951 FR239 1956 Replenish FR 239, 1976 Fair Morn FR 239
Admirality	Based Hong Kong, 30/4/64 sold at Singapore
Admirality	1946 Helen Herd FR141, 1947 Lebenon PD 392 1956 sank
Admirality	1947 Glenugie PD 340, 1956 sold to S. Africa
Admirality	20/7/60 Shalimar IV (Caernarvon) 1966 Yacht based Buckie
Admirality	1947 sold at Trincomalee
Admirality	at Hong Kong, 1957 Nan Lee, 1961 Hing Cheong, 1965 Shun Lee
Admirality	Based Borneo 1946 sold to Borneo Government
Admirality	1948 FPV Squirrel II 1956 sold to Malta, 1973 Tramp Gibralter
Admirality	1964 sold at Rochester as Meanderer
Admirality	1947 Margaret Herd FR 180, 1973 Shooting Star 1978?
Admirality	1946 Harvest Gleaner BCK 120, 1986 sold for Pleasure
Admirality	1946 Ashgrove A 244, 1957 PD 270, 1958 Spes Clara PD 270 1963 herring carrrier based at Shetland
J.Campbell Lossiemouth	1982 BS 27, 1986 based Padstow, 1987 ? No record
W.Thomson Lossiemouth	1952 no record in Olsen's Almanack
A.Reid Peterhead	
A.Campbell Lossiemouth	1960 Chary BF 228, 1967 BCK 243, 1995 Pleasure craft
J.Main Nairn	1963 based Ireland, 1977 B 184, 1982 N 384, 1993 Scrapped
J.Murray Lossiemouth	1965 PD 176, 1987 no record in Olsens almanack
Distributors Fishing Co	1960 no record in Olsens
Distributors Fishing Co	1959 Good Tidings PD 348, 1965 LK 680, 1985 GY 4 1987?
Wm Main Burghead	1960 N 160, 2002 Decommissioned Kilkeel
G.Campbell Lossiemouth	1980 based Fleetwood, 1984 no record in Olsens Almanack
A Farquhar Buckie	1973 Fruitful B 79, 1981 no record in Olsens Almanack
J.Clark Portessie	1963 Comet BCK 183, 1960's sank after collision off Wick
W.Murray Buckie	1960 Ann Kirk N 138, 1963 Castle BayN 138 1966 S 67.
Wm Smith Lossiemouth	1975 LH reg, 1981 no record in Olsens almanack
D Farquhar. Lossiemouth	1984 sold for pleasure based on the Thames
J.Phimister Findochty	1960 no record in Olsens
G Campbell Lossiemouth	1974 B 144,1986 FR 1990 no record in Olsens
D.McKenzie Burghead	1982 Based Fleetwood, 1986 no record in Olsens almanack
J.Ralph Hopeman	26th August Wrecked Gamrie Bay
A.Phimister Findochty	1974 N 217(R.Hanna Kilkeel) 1993 owner Sean Allan Kilkeel,
R.Herd Findochty	later Kathleen Anne BCK 77, 1984 sold to Ireland
J.Campbell Lossiemouth	Sank January Gale 1953 Crew rescued by Aberdeen Trawler
W.McKay Sandend	1970's sold for a wild life survey vessel on the Solent
Admirality	1959 based Hong Kong, 1967 broken up Hong Kong
Admirality	1969 Fishery Protection, 26-11-71 broken up at Portsmouth
Admirality	1962 sold to Libya renamed Zuara 1973 broken up
Admirality	1971 based Hong Kong (Patrol Duties P1055) 1984 broken up
J.Campbell Lossiemouth	1976 Ben Aigen INS 146, 1980no record in Olsens almanack
Admirality	1969 Thames, 1975 Woolaston, 1985 broken up Sittingbourne
M. McKay Lairg	1974 sold to Ireland W 91, 2002 no record found

No	Name	Reg No	Year	Dimensions (ft)	Power HP/KW	Tons
128	Estrolita	BCK 6	1954	73 x 19 x 9.3	152 / 113 Gardner	56
129	Kiloran	INS 220	1954	65 x 17.8 x 9.1	114 / 85 Gardner	
130	Acorn	INS 268	1954	69 x 19 x 9.6	152 / 113 Gardner	48
131	Green Pastures	BF 4	1954	39.99 x 14.90 x 6.80	66hp Kelvin	
132	Harvest Hope	PD 120	1954	39.9 x 14.9 x 6.8	66 /49 Kelvin	16
133	Green Pastures	N 20	1955	69.8 x 19.7 x 9.6	152 /113 Gardner	34
134	Effulgence	BF 24	1955	51.30 x 16.00 x 7.10	95hp Gardner	24
135	Havilah	N 12	1955	65.00 x 17.80 x 9.10	152hp Gardner	50
136	Susitna	GY 113	1955	65.10 x 18 x 8.9	152 / 113 Gardner	22
137	Guillemot	INS 304	1955	65.00 x 17.80 x 9.10	152hp Gardner	46
138	Albion	INS 305	1955	39.99 x 14.90 x 6.80	72hp Gardner	15
139	Margarita	BF 32	1955	69.9 x 18.10 x 9.6	152 / 113 Gardner	36
140	Suilven	BF 33	1955	51.30 x 16.00 x 7.10	95hp Gardner	24
141	Loch Kildonan	A 84	1956	100.80 x 22.00 x 11.00	335hp Ruston	149
142	Caledonia	INS 311	1955	69.99 x 19.70 x 9.6	152hp Gardner	50
143	Windermere II	PD 154	1956	71 x 19.7 x 9.6	152 Gardner	54
144	HMS Lewiston	CMS 108	1956	153ft x 28.90 x 14.90	3,000hp Napier Deltic	
145	Adoraim	PD158	1956	39.9 x15.37 x 5.74		14.68
146	Moyness	INS 124	1956	66.50 x 18.90 x 9.60	152hp Gardner	
147	Kyana	GY 232	1956	65.10 x 18 x 8.9	152 / 113 Gardner	22
148	Sar of Faith	PD 160	1956	71 x 19.7 x 9.6	152 / 113 Gardner	51
149	Coral Bank	GY 339	1956	63.10 x 17.6 x 9.1	105 / 78 Paxman	30
150	Viborg	H 33	1957	65.10 x 18 x 8.9	152 / 113 Gardner	51
151	Nordborg	H 35	1957	65.10 x 18 x 8.9	152 /113 Gardner	51
152	Green Hill	N 42	1957	68.00 x 19.70 x 9.60	152hp Gardner	
153	Ling Bank	GY 426	1957	63.10 x 17.6 x 9.1	105 / 78 Paxman	27
154	Liberty	INS 154	1956	66.5 x 18.9 x 9.6	152hp Gardner	49
155	Star of Loretta	A 186	1958	130 x 25 x 12.9	642hp Widdop	86
156	Alatna	GY 454	1958	65.10 x 19.7 x 8.6	152 / 113 Gardner	16
157	Opportune II	BCK 60	1957	69.9 x 19.1 x 9.6	152hp Gardner	49
158	Fragrant Rose	BCK 64	1957	73.09 x 20.42 x 8.21	152hp Gardner	49
159	Mayflower	INS 35	1957	65.40 x 18.48 x 8.58	152hp Gardner	45
160	Saxon II	GY 499	1958	65.10 x 18 x 8.9	152 / 113 Gardner	24
161	Olive leaf	INS 54	1957	69.9 x 19.7 x 9.6	152hp Gardner	52
162	Sandringham	GY 481	1958	65.10 x 18 x 8.9	152 / 113 Gardner	24
163	Vigilance	A 204	1958	109 x 22.7 x 12	454 / 338 Ruston	66
164	Sceptre	LK 377	1958	72.5 x 19.7 x 9.62	152hp Gardner	49
165	Strathyre	INS 65	1958	67 x 18.9 x 9.6	152 / 113 Gardner	45
166	Argosy	INS 66	1958	69.9 x 19.7 x 9.6	152hp Gardner	47
167	Britta	GY 595	1958	65.10 x 18 x 8.9	152 / 113 Gardner	24
168	Saxon King	GY 629	1959	65.10 x 18 x 8.9	152 / 113g	50
169	Castle Dawn	N 147	1959	69.9 x 19.7 x 9.6	152 / 113 Gardner	41
170	Rona Hansen	GY 599	1959	65.10 x 18 x 8.9	152 / 113 Gardner	23

Owner	History
W.B.Herd Findochty	1964 PD 145, 1968 sold to Ireland D 225, 2002 no record
J.C.Thomson Lossiemouth	1970 sold to Ireland D 228
W.Campbell Lossiemouth	1966 BCK 268. 1984 no record in Olsens
W. Wilson Portknockie	1961 Provider LH 435, 1963 TT 18, 1965 work boat Clair G
R.W.Stephens Boddam	1969 Tern CN 12, 1980 FY, 1983 Jeanie Marie RX 328, 1991?
W.V. Chambers Annalong	1966 no record to be found in Olsens Almanack
J.Gardiner Cullen	1963 Silver Cord BCK 200, 1976 AH 70, 1993 Pleasure craft
R.Donnan Holyhead	1965 Castle Vale N 12, 1973 WA 23, 1980 ? No record
V.Nielson Grimsby	1993 Decommissioned Grimsby
J.Young Hopeman	1967 Sapphire UL 194,
A Finlayson Nairn	1964 WK 88,1968 CN 45,1974 UL 145,1988 LH 170
G.Mair Portknockie	1974 Olive Leaf INS128,1976 WK 437,!985 SO 850,1997 ?
J.Cowie Portknockie	1974 Craigenroan BCK 93, 1975 / 76 sank off Mallaig
W.Stewart Aberdeen	1970 PD 79 , 17th January 1987 sank
J.C.Thomson Lossiemouth	1969 Caledonia Rose D 331
A.Reid Peterhead	1967Arctic SunsetFR386,1971Ocean StarFR386,1974INS173 1986 Gypsy Rose D 611, 1990 Windermere II MT 24
Admirality	1986 became target ship in Aberforth Missile Range Wales
A.Strachan Peterhead	later Starlight LK 366, 1984 A 47, 1987 based Tarbert 1999sold to Ireland 2005 based Derry as house boat
M.McIntosh Nairn	1970 PL 12, 1976 W 86
V.Nielson Grimsby	1962 no record found in Olsens Almanack
G. Nicol Peterhead	1967 sold to Ireland D 260.
Delga Fishing Co Grimsby	1993 no record found in Olsens
St Andrew Fishing Co Hull	1972 sank after collision with Icelandic vessel Manafoss
St Andrew Fishing Co Hull	1988 Mourne Endeavour N 235, 1996 Decommissioned
J.Chambers Annalong	
Delga Fishing Co Grimsby	1993 no record in Olsens Almanack
G.Young Hopeman	1979 B 282 J.Coffey Co Down, 2001 Decommissioned
Walker Steam fishing Co	1964 Admiral Mountbatton A 186, 1979 ? No record found
Alatna Seiners Cleethorpes	1993 Decommissioned Grimsby
G.Murray Buckie	1972 Saffron INS 95, 1982 Girvan, 1987 Portavogie 1994 scrap
W.J.Smith Portessie	1971 B 74, 1996 Mary Elizabeth FR 900, 2000 sold?
J.S.Liebnitz Lossiemouth	1985 Mayflower of Portavogie B 44
Forward Fishing Co grimsby	1978 sold. 1981 no record in Olsens Almanack
W.Thomson Lossiemouth	1975 no record
Queen Fishing Co Grimsby	1987 no record in Olsens
Devotion Fishing Co Aberdeen	1980 based lowestoft, 1981 engine removed became hulk
T.G.Fullerton Lerwick	1985 Avalon II WK 343, 1992 based Cornwall, 1997 scrapped
A.Souter Lossiemouth	2002 no record found in Fishing Vessels of UK
W.Campbell Lossiemouth	1974 Acorn INS 66, 1977 CN 220, 1989 B 84, 1993 Scrapped
L. Sorensen Ltd Grimsby	1982 no record in Olsens Almanack
Forward Fishing Co grimsby	1980 Delvan GY 629, 1995 no record in Olsens Almanack
R.Donnan Cloughey Co Down	1970 no record found in Olsens Almanack
Kowal Fishing Ltd Grimsby	1965 no record in Olsens Almanack

No	Name	Reg No	Year	Dimensions (ft)	Power HP/KW	Tons
171	Kytra	Yacht	1960	56 x 16 x 9.2		
172	Yukon Star	BCK 98	1959	72.8 x 19.10 x 9.6	240 / 178 Kelvin	56
173	Broadhaven	A 479	1959	102.4 x 22 x 11	454hp Ruston	163
174	Dreadnought	A 377	1959	102.4 x 22 x 11	454hp Ruston	163
175	Yukon Fisher	BCK 107	1959	72.8 x 19.10 x 9.6	240 / 178 Kelvin	55
176	Rosebloom	INS 94	1959	72.8 x 19.10 x 9.6	152hp Gardner	54
177	Green Isle	N 256	1959	73 x 19 x 9.3	152hp Gardner	44
178	Binks	GY 617	1959	58 x 15.10 x 9.6	114 / 85 Gardner	40
179	White Bank	GY 620	1960	58 x 15.10 x 9.6	133 / 99 Paxman	19
180	Honestas	LH 370	1960	70.5 x 19.1 x 8.6	152hp Gardner	49
181	Strathdoon	BA 122	1960	39.10 x 14.9 x 6.3	94 / 70 Gardner	16
182	Ben Loyal	UL 166	1960	69.9 x 19.10 x 9.6	152 / 113 Gardner	48
183	Cancelled					
184	Andvari	Yacht	1960	47.10 ft		
185	Rosemary	INS 116	1960	70 x 19.8 x 8.6	152hp Gardner	49
186	Tanana	GY 647	1960	58 x 15.10 x 9.6	114 / 85 Gardner	42
187	Ajax	INS 168	1962	74.4 x 19.8 x 9.6	200 / 149 Gardner	
188	Coral Princess	Cargo	1961	89.3 x 21 x 11	twin Gardners 300hp	
189	Edindoune	BCK 142	1960	37.75 ft	58hp Perkins	
190	Bennisan	GY 492	1961	58 x 15.10 x 9.6	155hp Rolls Royce	42
191	Ocean Venture	BF 263	1962	45 x 14.1 x 6.3	84hp Gardner	17.98
192	Rosemount	INS 177	1962	69.9 x 19.3 x 9.6	200 / 149 Gardner	
193	Marshira	Yacht	1961	37ft	86hp Parsons	
194	Astra Volante	Yacht	1961	56 x 16 x 9.2	158 Gardner	
195	Village Maid	CT 51	1961	50 x 17 x 8	150 Gardner	35
196	Arvor III	Yacht	1962	63 x 17.9 x 10.4	254 Gardner	
197	Ferrara	Yacht	1963	65 x 16 x 10	2x127 Gardner	
198	Scottish Simo	Yacht	1962	44.2 x 14.8 x 7	2x127 Gardner	
199	Skomer	Yacht	1963	56.2 x 16.4 x 9.0	152 Gardner	
200	Misty Isle	Yacht	1963	30.0 x 9.6 x 5	BMC	
201	Admirality	Target	1963			
202	Ella Rose	Yacht	1964	57.7 x 16.9 x 8.4	2x 254 Gardner	
203	Falcon	INS 235	1963	60.0 x 18.3 x 8	150 / 111 Gardner	34
204	R.N.L.I	Lifeboat	1966	37 x 11.5	Parsons	
205	R.N.L.I	Lifeboat	1966	37 x 11.5	Parsons	
206	Rizq-al-Bahr	FRV vessel	1964	67 x 20.3 x 10.6	320 Kelvin	
207	Ardelle	BCK 227	1964	74.6 x 20.4 x 9.05	Mercedes	57.65
208	Ambitious	N 190	1965	69.3 x 20.25 x 9.6	200 Gardner	50.86
209	Green Pastures II	N 210	1965	74.11 x 22.25 x 9.6	380 Caterpiller	52.42
210	Covesea	INS 307	1965	62.6 x 18.5 x 8	200 / 149 Gardner	23.29
211	Golden Strand	BF 403	1966	50 x 15.7 x 7.6	180 / 134 Caterpiller	25

Owner

History

Owner	History
G.Goodsbody Inverness	1980's American owner based Troon.
Bantry Fishing Cleethorpes	1964 Athabasca FD 242, 1974 Our Van Clare GY 288
Faithlee Fishing Co	1972 no record in Olsens could be sold abroad
Grampian Fishing Co	1984 Putford Harrier (aircraft recovery & stand by) sold 1992
Bantry Fishing Cleethorpes	1965 Matanuska FD 243, 1970 D 523, 1975 no record ?
T.Ross Burghead	1985 wrecked Denmark
V.Chambers Annalong	1974 D 52, 1997 no record in Fishing vessels of UK & Ireland
Loumand Fishing Co Grimsby	1996 Decommissioned
Delga Fishing Co Grimsby	1990 no record found in Olsens Almanack
W.Cairnie Edinburgh	1967 KY 370, 1972 INS 32, 1985 Ardmore PD 107, 1994 Yacht
A. Smith Ayr.	1973 Boy David TT 78, 1996 Decommissioned Carradale
J.Stewart Lossiemouth	1981 WK 3, 1992 based Newlyn.
Cancelled	
J.H.MacKenzie Fochabers	2006 seen lying ashore on her side in mud at Penryn
W.Garden Lossiemouth	1976 WK 412, 1982 Alliance INS 271, 1983 B 15, 1996 N 305
Neilson Fishing Co Grimsby	2002 Decommissioned Grimsby
W.Campbell Lossiemouth	1967 Orion BCK 69, 1975 Talisman PD 158, 1980's sank off Orkney not long after a major refit
for Soloman Islands	
J.H. MacKenzie Fochabers	later Horizon SY 294, 1990's based at Connel near Oban
bellavie Fishing Co Grimsby	2001 G 431 Based Galway, 2005 no record ?
J.Watt Gardenstown	1974 Sincerity II AH 58, 1983 LH 188,
D. Mitchell Lossiemouth	1975 BCK 277, 1985 Golden gain FR 59, 1991 Alice Louise FZ592 1997 scrapped
A webb Anglesay	
Sir John Grady	1998 renamed Leonor II based Barcelona Spain
W.C.Watterson Isle of Man	1973 Village Maid SO 315
Francois Ouvre, Paris	1995 owner Mark Tyler Sheldon Gloucester New England
Mr D. Crudsen, Faringdon	
Wing Commander Spier ,	Nairn
Major St John Plevins	sold Now Based at Tasmania
Mr F.Jones, Colwyn Bay	
Admirality	
Mr S. Bourne	
J.Sutherland Hopeman	1974 Favour Ins 235, 1994/95 decommissioned
R.N.L.I	
R.N.L.I	
Dept of Fisheries Aden	
W.B.Herd Findochty	1976 ownerW.J.Cowie,1980's J.Herd,1998 T.Mearns,1999 John Mitchell Whitehills, 2002 decommissioned Macduff
E.McKee Kilkeel	1994 owner S.Cully Portavogie, 1997 reregistered B 420
V.Chambers Annalong	1977 / 2002 various owners 2002 for sale in yacht magazine
J.Campbell Lossiemouth	1976 Shannon IV INS 307, 1983 N 307, 1989 Mark A INS 137, 1991 valour B289, 1996 D476 besed Arklow, 2002 no record
C.Mair Cullen.	1974 SY 173,1977 no record, 1986 in Norwegian Almanack as Seljefish H-5-0, 1985 Kystifisk H-5-0, 1990 TK-19-K

No	Name	Reg No	Year	Dimensions (ft)	Power HP/KW	Tons
212	Victory	INS 224	1966	63.3 x 19.2 x 8.6	150 / 111 Gardner	44.4
213	Flourish II	INS 123	1966	61.6 x 18.4 x 7.8	200 / 149 Gardner	37.59
214	Pemberton	Yacht	1967	47 x 15.25 x 6.5	172 Gardner	
215	Fair Morn	BA 295	1966	61.6 x 18.4 x 7.8	200 / 149 Caterpiller	37.32
216	Admirality	Target	1966			
217	Comet III	BCK 242	1967	75 x 20.4 x 9	Mercedes	46.84
218	Janeen	BCK 5	1968	50 x 15.9 x 6.2	210 / 156 Caterpiller	20.75
219	Olbek	GY 1389	1967	65.10 x 18.5 x 6.95	200 / 149 Gardner	49
220	Helena	BCK 248	1967	71.7 x 20.3 x 8.8	200 / 149 Gardner	51.54
221	Seafire	UL 260	1967	63.3 x 19.3 x 8.6	180 / 134 Caterpiller	44.29
222	Caberfeidh	Yacht	1967	30 x 9.6 x 4.7	36 Mercedes	
223	Ajax	INS 168	1968	77.1 x 22.3 x 9.9	380 / 283 Caterpiller	70.93
224	Marandi	Yacht	1968	47 x 14.1 x 6.5		
225	New Dawn	BA 18	1968	64.10 x 19.0 x 8.1	345 / 257 Caterpiller	42.31
226	Green Valley	N 20	1969	75 x 21.25 x 9.4	425 / 316 Caterpiller	89.56
227	Monadhliath	INS 140	1968	59.6 x 19 x 8.6	200 / 149 Gardner	36
228	Horizon	INS 21	1969	78 x 22.3 x 9.8	400 / 298 Caterpiller	71
229	Sunrise	UL 66	1969	65 x 19.35 x 7.32	200 / 149 Gardner	39
230	Heathery Brae	BF 26	1969	54.3 x 17.4 x 6.25	172 / 128 Gardner	24.51
231	Pacemaker	GY 165	1970	54.3 x 17.5 x 6.25	150 / 111 Gardner	25
232	Minerva	BCK 24	1970	71.3 x 20.5 x 7.6	230 / 171 Gardner	46.77
233	Scarlet Line	LH 55	1970	78 x 22.4 x 9.6	400 / 298 Kelvin	69.09
234	Alkaid	INS 102	1970	65 x 19.4 x 6.85	230 / 171 Gardner	36.9
235	Captain Scott	Schooner	1971	144.3 x 28 x	2x230 Gardner	
236	Seaforth	BCK 177	1971	73.6 x 21.4 x 7.65	425 / 316 Caterpiller	49.62
237	not built	Yacht				
238	Monadhliath	INS 140	1971	64 x 19.2 x 6.9	230 / 171 Gardner	35.5
239	Seagull	BF 74	1971	56 x 18.55 x 5.75	365 /272 Caterpiller	26.93
240	Unity	BCK 57	1972	56 x 18.55 x 5.9	300 / 223 Caterpiller	24.43
241	Lairlochie	GY 213	1972	54 x 17.5 x 5.35	150 / 111 Gardner	21
242	Macandi	GY 220	1972	66 x 18.6 x 7.35	200 / 149 Gardner	24
243	Silver Spray	BCK 87	1972	56 x 18.6 x 5.8	300 / 223 Volvo	24.56
244	Golden Splendour	INS 63	1973	80 x 23.4 x 8.2	500 / 372 Caterpiller	64.85
245	Celnius	BCK 151	1973	56 x 18.6 x 5.8	300 / 223 Caterpiller	24.49
246	Ocean Trust	BF 307	1973	74 x 22 x 7.5	575 / 428 Brit.Polar	49
247	Laurisa	BA 145	1973	56 x 18.6 x 9.35	230 / 171 Gardner	24.46
248	Lynn Marie	BCK 86	1973	56.2 x 18.4 x 6.2	270 / 201 Volvo	24.07
249	Marandi	Yacht	1973	63 x 19.1 x 9.35	2x 176 Gardner	
250	Kesteven	GY 277	1973	54 x 17.5 x 6.2	150 / 111 Gardner	25
251	Morning Star	BCK 10	1974	56 x 18.6 x 6.2	300 / 223 Caterpiller	25.44
252	Margarita	BCK 32	1974	74.8 x 21.2 x 7.4	425 / 316 Caterpiller	49.21

Owner	History
G.Fennel Lossiemouth	1980 Embrace INS 224, 1994 Decommissioed in Ireland
J.M.Sutherland Hopeman	1992 N 123, (Austin Crawford Kilkeel) 1994 Decommissioned
Mr Rigby, Caernarvon	
A.Munro Ayr	1983 Anna Bhan INS 319 (R.Souter Buckie) 1994 scrapped
Admirality	
R Phimister Findochty	1971 Arcturus, 1976 Marina, 1994 Confide BF 324 1999 sold to Montrose for Sea Anglisng Vessel
J.Smith Buckie	1975 LK 277, 1980 A 677, 1986 N 91, 1988 LO 81
L.Sorenson Ltd Grimsby	2004 no record in Fishing vessel of UK & Ireland
J.Strachan Portessie	1976 Marlene, 1981 Aquarius INS 286, 1994 scrapped
J.Main Nairn	1977 Freedom III BA 280
J.H.MacKenzie	renamed Eva
W.Campbell Lossiemouth	1973 Harvest Hope PD 96,1976 Star of Bethlehem PD 96, 1987 Opportunus, 1995 Benaiah III N841, 1997 scrapped.
J.H.MacKenzie	
J.Munro Ayr	2002 Decommissioned at loch Ryan
T.H.Chambers Annalong	1977 GY 299, 1983 INS 9, 1995 Decommissioned
A.Jack Avoch	1970 sank in the minch after calor gas explosion
J.Thomson Lossiemouth	1979 BCK 212, 1988 FR 261, 1996 Decommissioned
J.Campbell Lossiemouth	1976 owner J.Coull Findochty, 1980's wrecked West Coast
A.Innes Portknockie	1988 Kildonan UL 145, (R.MacGregor Ullapool)
Delga Fishing Co Grimsby	
A.McKay Buckie	1986 FR 147, 1988 Margaret Anne INS 130, 1997 Osprey, 2003 Decommissioned
G.Buchannan Port Seton	1986 Charisma FR 75, 1998 sold to Eire Charisma G 220
G.Main Hopeman	1983 Alvidra Elaine WK 111,1996 Strathdonnan WK 111, 1997 Rhodunna B14.
Dulverton Trust	Later sold to Oman renamed Shabab Oman (youth of Oman)
Harbourhead Fishing Co	1987 Amity PD 177, 1997 sold to Eire Amity S 233
G.Moffat USA	
A.Jack Avoch	2002 converted to pleasure registered Strande German owner
K. West Macduff	1982 sold Ireland DA 3, 1987 BCK 62, 2001 Sustain BCK 62
W.J.Smith Buckie	1986 Silver Star FR 73, 1988 BCK 131, 2002 scrapped
Delga Fishing Co Grimsby	1993 / 94 Decommissioned
Delga Fishing Co Grimsby	1993 / 94 Decommissioned
W.A.Coull Buckie	1983 Silver Star KY 154,1989 Ajax AH 32, 1990 based St Ives
T.Ross Burghead	1994 owner G.McLean PD,1997 G 222 Galway, 2002 ?
W.J.Mair Buckie	1988 Tenacious BCK 119, 1993 Dalriada BCK 180, 1998 Sarah Joan LK 987, 2003 scrapped
J.Watt & others Aberdeen	1980 owner J.Hay Cullen, 1986 sold to Sweden, 1993 Ostanvag, 2001 Vingasand SM154, 2002 Rio LL775
J.H.Gibson Maidens	1981 Green Brae INS 208
Wm. Wilson Portessie	
J.H.MacKenzie	
Delga Fishing Co Grimsby	1995/96 Decommissioned Grimsby
C.Mair Cullen.	1995 based aberdeen, 2003 /04 Decommissioned Denmark
L.G.Mair Buckie	1992 Atlantic Star PD 322, 1997 Decommissioned Ireland

No	Name	Reg No	Year	Dimensions (ft)	Power HP/KW	Tons
253	Hazelmore	BCK 63	1974	74 x 21.3 x 7.4	425 / 316 Caterpiller	49.5
254	Arnborg	H 272	1974	54 x 17.5 x 6.2	150 / 111 Gardner	21.35
255	Vikingborg	H 285	1974	54 x 17.5 x 6.2	150 / 111 Gardner	21.76
256	Wave Crest	BCK 217	1974	56 x 18.6 x 6.5	300 / 223 Volvo	26.5
257	Copious	BF 237	1975	74.7 x 21.3 x 7.52	500 / 372 Kelvin	49.94
258	Helenus	UL 66	1975	56 x 18.4 x 5.9	300 / 223 Caterpiller	24.57
259	Heather Sprig	BCK 153	1975	55.3 x 18.7 x 5.9	300 / 223 Kelvin	24.3
260	Janeen II	BCK 29	1976	55.6 x 18.3 x 5.6	300 / 223 Kelvin	22.5
261	not built					
262	Moravia	INS 86	1975	71.20 x 20.0 x 6.9	230 / 171 Gardner	42.04
263	Edlei	GY 455	1975	66 x 18.6 x 6.7	230 / 171 Gardner	22.44
264	Joysona	BCK 148	1976	75.4 x 21.7 x 7.3	500 / 372 Kelvin	49.82
265	Green Field	N 57	1977	87.2 x 24.1 x 12.4	800 / 596 Blackstone	76
266	Green Isle II	N 64	1977	87 x 24.15 x 12.4	800 / 596 Blackstone	76
267	Julie Anne	BCK 140	1977	74.75 x 21.25 x 7.3	500 / 372 Kelvin	48.8
268	St Kilda	INS 47	1978	79.7 x 23.7 x 10.1	725 / 540 Caterpiller	80.79
269	Bounteous	BCK 337	1978	54.9 x 18.5 x 5.7	310 / 231 Kelvin	23.63
270	Accord	FR 262	1978	69 x 22.2 x 6.9	500 / 372 Kelvin	44.18
271	Harmony	INS 257	1978	74.2 x 21 x 7.4	500 / 372 Kelvin	48.81
272	Crystal Sea	LH 97	1979	54.9 x 18.6 x 5.7	365 / 272 Caterpiller	23.66
273	Heritage	INS 247	1979	64.40 x 21.9 x 7.4	415 / 309 Kelvin	44.77
274	Coel-Na-Mara	BF 352	1979	55.5 x 18.6 x 5.8	365 / 272 Caterpiller	23.93
275	Wendy Pulfrey	BCK 198	1979	79.3 x 23.52 x 9.04	415 / 309 Kelvin	71.17
276	Silent Waters	N 344	1980	56.4 x 18.5 x 6.7	328 / 244 Volvo	50grt
277	Star Award	BF 407	1980	56.3 x 18.41 x 5.67	415 / 310 Kelvin	23.49
278	Flourish II	LK 450	1980	56.3 x 18.3 x 5.45	290 / 216 Volvo	22.84
279	not built					
280	Avoca	BCK 294	1981	75.33 x 21.54 x 7.45	415 / 309 Kelvin	49.69
281	Providence	BF 422	1982	59.78 x 20.93 x 7.7	470 / 350 Cummins	39.05
282	Silver Fern	FR 416	1982	59.1 x 20.66 x 8.10	495 / 370 Kelvin	37.41
283	Kelly	BCK 303	1982	59.96 x 20.72 x 8.15	328 / 244 Volvo	40.4
284	Hazelmore II	BCK 83	1983	75.90 x 21.18 x 7.45	495 / 369 Caterpiller	49.67
285	Bunillidh	WK 96	1984	63.50 x 22.11 x 8.2	400 / 298 Caterpiller	48.82
286	Radiant Way	LH 147	1984	59.12 x 19.12 x 7.97	310 / 231 Kelvin	37.24
287	Loch Inchard II	UL 44	1984	60.1 x 21.25 x 7.61	360 / 262 Volvo	39.37
288	Ptarmigan	BCK 26	1984	75.88 x 21.06 x 7.41	495 / 369 Kelvin	49.68
289	Aquilla II	BCK 43	1986	65.58 x 22.14 x 8.05	400 / 298 Caterpiller	49.11
290	Unity II	BCK 35	1986	61.22 x 22.27 x 8.3	495 / 369 Caterpiller	44.65
291	Hope	BCK 59	1986	65.3 x 22.47 x 7.6	310 / 231 Gardner	47.47
292	Bonaventure	LH 111	1987	71.2 x 22.01 x 8.39	495 / 369 Caterpiller	55.33
293	Rebecca	LH 11	1987	67.74 x 22.17 x 7.93	495 / 369 Caterpiller	49.99
294	Eleanda	BCK 60	1988	75.59 x 23.19 x 8.00	650 / 484 Kelvin	59.48

Owner	History
W.B.More Buckie	1983 Harmony LK 63, 2001 scrapped
Boston Deep Sea Co Hull	Various owners since built but same registration
Boston Deep Sea Co Hull	Various owners since built but same registration
George Campbell Findochty	1998--2001 various owners, 2006 Ocean Way FR 349
W.McKay Sandend	1995 Opportunus PD 96, 2002 scrapped Denmark
A.Farquhar Portknockie	1987 Strathelliot A 446,1998 Ben Loyal A 875, 2003 scrapped
J.Smith Buckie	1988 Kemarvin BF 4, 2006 WK 814
J.Smith Buckie	2003 Decommissioned Denmark
Garden Portessie	
J.C.Thompson Lossiemouth	1981 Moray View INS 86, 1996 Heritage B 786
Edlei Fishing Co Grimsby	
J.Humphrey Buckie	1982 Dayspring PD 288, 1996 sold to Eire Dayspring D 660
V.Chambers Annalong	1984 (Norway) Gullaks H-26-FE, 1989 Brodrene Husevag, 1997 Gunnerson M70-M, 2000 Nordnes, 2000 Ronaldnes
V.Chambers Annalong	1984 sold to Norway Soloyvag M-112-F 2003 no record found
J.Smith Buckie	1985 Three Sisters FR 96, 2000 based Mallaig,2001 scrapped
J.C.Thompson Lossiemouth	1992 Quo Vive FR 201,1998 Dalriada BF 262, 2003 scrapped
E.Phimister Buckie	1982 Galeen BCK 337, 1993 Lauralena BCK 367, 1997 S 262
W.McKay Fraserburgh	1989 Accord BCK 262
A.McPherson Hopeman	1995 sold to Eire Reg D 207
A.B.Johnston Port Seton	1997 Fraoch Ban LK 966, 15/8/99 sank off Shetland
A.Flett Hopeman	1990 FR 254, 1994 LK 373 1998 Golden Emblem B 908
A Watt Gardenstown	1998 K 1003, 2005 Shekinah INS 155
Riverside Trawlers Grimsby	1995 Silver Line GY 36 2002 Decommissioned
McKee Kilkeel	1983 BF 258, 1990 Star O'Orkney, 1992 Silent Waters, 2002 decommissioned
M.Slater Macduff	1986 AH 77,1997 based Whitby, 2001 Star of Hope FR 200, 2005 based Portavogie, 2007 Cathzelle B222
Kay Shetland	1992 Heathery Brae IV BF 87, 1999 Leandra K, 2001Primrose II
D.Campbell Findochty	2002 Decommissioned at Macduff
D.Watt Gardenstown	1995 owner G.West, 1998 Seaway PD 319, 1999 Headway, 2002 Headway BF856 (R Calvin Whitehaven)
A.G.Wiseman Fraserburgh	
Danbrit Fishing Co Grimsby	1989--2005 various owners 2005 DS 7, 2006 BCK 625
W.B.More Buckie	1991 Ocean Reward BCK 83, 1997 Aurora BF 812, 1999 sank
D.Cowie Helmsdale	1999 Achieve FR 100
K Dawson Seahouses	1996 Crystal Stream LH 147 (A.Johnston Port Seton)
J.M.R.McKay Kinlochbervie	
D.A.Goodbrand	2000 Christine K PD 306, 2003 decommissioned Denmark
E Simpson Buckie	1992 Chrisona BF 361, 1999 Bountiful BF 79
J.Flett Buckie	1993 Caledonia BCK 35 (Edwin Clarke Portknockie), 2007 Aubretia BCK32
L.G.McKay Buckie	1998 FR 906 (K.Stuart Fraserburgh) 2001 sank off Aberdeen
T.I.Bain Eyemouth	1994 sold to B.Blackie Eyemouth
R.Miller Musselburgh	1994 Heatherbelle VI LH 272, 1998 Rebecca LH 11
D.Main Buckie	1992 Kevella BF 364, 2000 sold to Eire Atlantic Fisher T 116

No	Name	Reg No	Year	Dimensions (ft)	Power HP/KW	Tons
295	Stelimar	CY 163	1988	40.28 x 16.01 x 6.6	182 / 135 Gardner	18.25
296	Guiding Light	CY 127	1988	40.28 x 16.01 x 6.6	182 / 135 Gardner	19.17
297	Germount	K 970	1989	49.2 x 17.48 x 10.3	230 / 171 Cummins	15.5
298	Aquaria	K 232	1990	51.1 x 17.48 x 10.33	374 / 275 Gardner	29.44
299	Laurel	PL 6	1990	54.59 x 18.50 x 10.49	310 / 231 Gardner	38.77
300	Egalite	K 366	1991	49.11 x 17.00 x 8.00	250 / 179 Cummins	15.51
301	Julie	BF 211	1991	39.13 x 15.18 x 8.64	250 / 179 Gardner	19.26
	F.M.A.	(Herd	and	Mackenzie)	Yard	taken
506	Mizpah	BF 777	1994	84.6 x 26.3 x 17.00	981 / 732 Deutz	158.8
505	Crystal River	BF 32	1994	68.22 x 24.92 x 12.79	706 / 527 Deutz	88.92
507	Paragon V	PD 786	1995	81.40 x 26.01 x 19.35	960 / 716 Caterpiller	175.2
		Jones		went into	Receivership	and
508	Copious	BF 237	1996	79.70 x 25.91 x 15.74	854 / 637 Deutz	214.3
509	Loch Aline	Ferry	1997			
510	Antares	BF 27	2001	54.79 x 20.34 x 11.81	480 / 358 Caterpiller	44.12
511	Pleiades	BF 155	2001	54.79 x 20.34 x 11.81	480 / 358 Caterpiller	44.1
512	Holly B	FR 29	2001	57.74 x 20.99 x 11.81	583 / 434 Caterpiller	46.68
513	Fram IV	BRD	2005	32.48 x 17.06 x 4.2		
	Vessels	Built	at	Peterhead	Yard	
127	Sealgair	WK 241	1954	65 x 17.8 x 9.1	152 / 113 Gardner	48
128	Estrolita	BCK 6	1954	73 x 19 x 9.3	152 / 113 Gardner	56
129	Kiloran	INS 220	1954	65 x 17.8 x 9.1	114 / 85 Gardner	
130	Acorn	INS 268	1954	69 x 19 x 9.6	152 / 113 Gardner	48
132	Harvest Hope	PD 120	1954	39.9 x 14.9 x 6.8	66 / 49 Kelvin	16
133	Green Pastures	N 20	1955	69.8 x 19.7 x 9.6	152 / 113 Gardner	34
136	Susitna	GY 113	1955	65.10 x 18 x 8.9	152 / 113 Gardner	22
139	Margarita	BF 32	1955	69.9 x 18.10 x 9.6	152 / 113 Gardner	36
143	Windermere II	PD 154	1956	71 x 19.7 x 9.6	152 Gardner	54
143					152 / 113 Gardner	
145	Adoraim	PD158	1956	39.9 x15.37 x 5.74		14.68
147	Kyana	GY 232	1956	65.10 x 18 x 8.9	152 / 113 Gardner	22
148	Sar of Faith	PD 160	1956	71 x 19.7 x 9.6	152 / 113 Gardner	51
149	Coral Bank	GY 339	1956	63.10 x 17.6 x 9.1	105 / 78 Paxman	30
150	Viborg	H 33	1957	65.10 x 18 x 8.9	152 / 113 Gardner	51
151	Nordborg	H 35	1957	65.10 x 18 x 8.9	152 /113 Gardner	51
153	Ling Bank	GY 426	1957	63.10 x 17.6 x 9.1	105 / 78 Paxman	27
156	Alatna	GY 454	1958	65.10 x 19.7 x 8.6	152 / 113 Gardner	16
160	Saxon II	GY 499	1958	65.10 x 18 x 8.9	152 / 113 Gardner	24
162	Sandringham	GY 481	1958	65.10 x 18 x 8.9	152 / 113 Gardner	24
163	Vigilance	A 204	1958	109 x 22.7 x 12	454 / 338 Ruston	66

Owner

History

D.F.Macrae Grimsay	2002 sold to Iain Johnston Grimsay
D. Stewart Grimsay	
I.Richardson Stromness	1990 owner J.Peace Rousay, 2002 owner D MacMillan Uist
I.Richardson Stromness	1990 owner E.Sinclair Stromness, 1999 owner D Stewart Uist
G.R.Comber Peel	1998 KY 986, 2004 LK 227, 2005 CY 341
I.Richardson Stromness	1993 owner N.Matheson Stromness, 1994 B.Sutherland, Hopeman, 2004 Nordic Way FR 973
Ian McKay Findochty	1995 Kelly Ann II OB 156
over by Jones Shipyard	
Robert Mitchell Macduff	
B.Robertson Portknockie	2000 Aquarius BF 89 (Scott Shepherd Macduff)
James Thain Peterhead	fitted out at Richard Dunston Hull, 1998 Starlight PD 786
were taken over by	**Lithgow Group - renamed Buckie Shipyard**
W.& I McKay Portsoy	
Cal Mac Ferry's Gourock	
John Hepburn Fraserburgh	
Gary & Phillip Hepburn	2007 Caledonia II BCK 35
Ian Bruce Fraserburgh	2004 Ajax FR 29
Kenny Livingston Sheildaig	
M. McKay Lairg	1974 sold to Ireland W 91, 2002 no record found
W.B.Herd Findochty	1964 PD 145, 1968 D 225, 2002 no record
J.C.Thomson Lossiemouth	1970 sold to Ireland D 228
W.Campbell Lossiemouth	1966 BCK 268. 1984 no record in Olsens
R.W.Stephens Boddam	1969 Tern II CN 12,1980 FY,1983 Jeanie Marie RX 328
W.V. Chambers Annalong	1966 no record to be found in Olsens Almanack
V.Nielson Grimsby	1993 Decommissioned Grimsby
G.Mair Portknockie	1974 Olive Leaf INS 128, 1976 WK437, 1985 SO 850, 1997 ?
A.Reid Peterhead	1967 Arctic Sunset FR386, 1971 Ocean Star, 1974 INS 173
	1986 Gypsy Rose D 611, 1990 Windermere II MT 24, 1993 decommissioned Grimsby
A.Strachan Peterhead	later Starlight LK 366, 1984 A 47, 1987 based Tarbert Argyll, 1999 baed Ireland, 2005 converted Houseboat at Derry
V.Nielson Grimsby	1962 no record found in Olsens Almanack
G. Nicol Peterhead	1967 sold to Ireland D 260.
Delga Fishing Co Grimsby	1993 no record found in Olsens
St Andrew Fishing Co Hull	1973 no record in Olsens Almanack
St Andrew Fishing Co Hull	1988 Mourne Endeavour N 235, 1996 Decommissioned
Delga Fishing Co Grimsby	1993 no record in Olsens Almanack
Alatna Seiners Cleethorpes	1993 Decommissioned Grimsby
Forward Fishing Co grimsby	1978 sold. 1981 no record in Olsens Almanack
Queen Fishing Co Grimsby	1987 no record in Olsens
Devotion Fishing Co Aberdeen	1982 no record in Olsens Almanack

No	Name	Reg No	Year	Dimensions (ft)	Power HP/KW	Tons
165	Strathyre	INS 65	1958	67 x 18.9 x 9.6	152 / 113 Gardner	45
167	Britta	GY 595	1958	65.10 x 18 x 8.9	152 / 113 Gardner	24
168	Saxon King	GY 629	1959	65.10 x 18 x 8.9	152 / 113g	50
169	Castle Dawn	N 147	1959	69.9 x 19.7 x 9.6	152 / 113 Gardner	41
170	Rona Hansen	GY 599	1959	65.10 x 18 x 8.9	152 / 113 Gardner	23
172	Yukon Star	BCK 98	1959	72.8 x 19.10 x 9.6	240 / 178 Kelvin	56
175	Yukon Fisher	BCK 107	1959	72.8 x 19.10 x 9.6	240 / 178 Kelvin	55
178	Binks	GY 617	1959	58 x 15.10 x 9.6	114 / 85 Gardner	40
179	White Bank	GY 620	1960	58 x 15.10 x 9.6	133 / 99 Paxman	19
181	Strathdoon	BA 122	1960	39.10 x 14.9 x 6.3	94 / 70 Gardner	16
182	Ben Loyal	UL 166	1960	69.9 x 19.10 x 9.6	152 / 113 Gardner	48
186	Tanana	GY 647	1960	58 x 15.10 x 9.6	114 / 85 Gardner	42
187	Ajax	INS 168	1962	74.4 x 19.8 x 9.6	200 / 149 Gardner	
190	Bennisan	GY 492	1961	58 x 15.10 x 9.6	155hp Rolls Royce	42
191	Ocean Venture	BF 263	1962	45 x 14.1 x 6.3	84hp Gardner	17.98
192	Rosemount	INS 177	1962	69.9 x 19.3 x 9.6	200 / 149 Gardner	

Owner	History
A.Souter Lossiemouth	2002 no record found in Fishing Vessels of UK
L. Sorensen Ltd Grimsby	1982 no record in Olsens Almanack
Forward Fishing Co grimsby	1980 Delvan GY 629, 1995 no record in Olsens Almanack
R.Donnan Cloughey Co Down	1970 no record found in Olsens Almanack
Kowal Fishing Ltd Grimsby	1965 no record in Olsens Almanack
Bantry Fishing Cleethorpes	1964 Athabasca FD 242, 1974 Our Van Clare GY 288, 1994 ?
Bantry Fishing Cleethorpes	1965 Matanuska FD 243, 1970 D 523, 1975 no record found
Loumand Fishing Co Grimsby	1996 Decommissioned
Delga Fishing Co Grimsby	1990 no record found in Olsens Almanack
A. Smith Ayr.	1973 Boy David TT 78, 1996 Decommissioned Carradale
J.Stewart Lossiemouth	1981 WK 3, 1992 based Newlyn.
Neilson Fishing Co Grimsby	2002 Decommissioned Grimsby
W.Campbell Lossiemouth	1967 Orion BCK 69, 1975 Talisman PD 158, 1980's sank
bellavie Fishing Co Grimsby	2001 G 431 based Galway, 2005 no record found
J.Watt Gardenstown	1974 Sincerity II AH 58, 1983 LH 188
D. Mitchell Lossiemouth	1975 BCK 277, 1985 Golden Gain FR 59, 1991 Alice Louise PZ592, 1997 scrapped

Notes